Family Court: Giving Evidence In Family Court

By Michael D Watson

ISBN: 978-1-5272-7664-2

Contents

Essential Giving Evidence Checklist Access 5

Introduction 7

Legal Information For Parents 21

Parenting 61

Responsibility 91

Controlling Your Emotions 105

Self-Analysis Questions 131

Mastery Of Detail 139

Giving Evidence In Court 147

Cross-Examination 159

Case Studies 179

The 'Do's And Dont's' Of Giving Evidence 299

Conclusion 327

Essential Giving Evidence Checklist 333

Profile 335

Essential Giving Evidence Checklist Access

As a thank you for purchasing a copy of my book, you have also gained free access to my Essential Giving Evidence Checklist.

This essential checklist is designed to help you:

1. Prepare more thoroughly
2. Present more competently and more confidently.
3. Give more focused answers
4. To recognise it is imperative to master your emotions

You can download this vital checklist today at the following link: www.familycourttips.co.uk

You can contact me at:

Follow me on social media:

Facebook

Instagram

Twitter

LinkedIn

You Tube

Introduction

You are presumably reading this book because you need, or have been requested, to attend court for the purpose of giving evidence, and consequently require as much vital information as possible about what the process entails, and how best to prepare for your impending court date.

If this is the first time you've been asked to attend court, you are highly likely to experience the process as an extremely daunting one. But even if you have been required to stand in the witness box on several occasions previously, you will, I think, be only too well aware how anxiety-provoking and stressful the process can be.

Perhaps the best way to describe the experience of giving evidence (if you have never done so before) is to relate it to an interview situation. Except that, what is at stake is far greater than whether you are offered the job or not. In addition, the nature of the court environment is adversarial (or one of conflict) where the person firing questions at you is well prepared, skilled, and often very experienced at what they do.

It is the job of the person cross-examining you (i.e. your opponent's barrister or lawyer) to use all their knowledge, skill, experience, effort and means at their disposal to discredit you in the eyes of the judge. To rubbish, ridicule, undermine or negate your argument or account of what has taken place, and to seek to portray you negatively, or in such a way as to make their client's case stronger or more convincing, at your expense.

Given that this is their job, that they are engaged in daily, and they have been professionally trained to do this work, I think you can quickly grasp that even if you have attended court as a lay person (a person, parent or social worker not legally trained) on numerous occasions, that the person cross-examining you, is as far ahead of you as a professional sprinter would likely be, in the event you chose to compete with them in a 100 metres race.

There is then, for you no 'level playing field' when you are thrust into the court arena, and are up against lawyers and barristers. The odds are quite clearly stacked against you as a lay person and it does not matter how bright, educated or naturally articulate you are. The reality is that for you to have a chance of competing properly within the arena of the family court, you need exposure to, and indeed to be immersed in, that type of specialised knowledge, to enable you to defend yourself adequately."

Please do not think for one second, that your inability to perform on a 'level playing field' with your opponent's legal representative has necessarily anything to do with your level of intelligence.

It does not.

You have to bear in mind, in fact, burn it into your memory, that people who cross-examine you, not only have received specialised knowledge and training, but they live, breathe and thrive in an environment, which is totally alien to the average person. The court environment is really akin to being in another world entirely.

Outside on the streets, people do battle via abusing others with their mouths (abuse and profanity), fists and (sadly) with physical weapons.

In the courtroom, battle is waged in a totally different way, involving a different set of rules, expectations (often referred to as court etiquette) and weaponry. Although the weapons used are not physical ones, the arsenal at their disposal can be every bit as lethal as physical weapons, since people can be emotionally ripped to pieces, and reduced to quivering wrecks whilst in the witness box.

The overall impact on you, is often a traumatic one, and the implications arising from the outcome of your court case, may engender longer term difficulties, which affect your wellbeing and quality of life, for yourself and those you love.

So, if you agree with me that, for the likes of you and other lay people, it is not a ‘level playing field,’ and that the court environment is an alien one, then a reasonable question you might ask is: “how do I get the knowledge or develop the skills to improve the odds in my favour?”

The only way you are going to develop the required skills, is either to put yourself through the misery and burden of numerous court trials, and hope to pick them up, or alternatively find someone who possesses that level of specialist knowledge, relevant to giving evidence and being cross-examined, and learn it from them.

In my view, (and as I argue below) it is not at all easy to find someone who possesses the level of skills you require, and it is for this reason that I have chosen to write this book.

This would seem to be an appropriate time, to share with you some information about the author, that I hope will be useful to you. It will amongst other things, explain why I consider I am an expert in this area, and why I believe I am extremely well placed to write this book, and offer you the opportunity of familiarising yourself with the specialised knowledge and expertise that I have spent the last thirty plus years of my life honing.

I should say from the outset that I am not legally trained, although I have acted as an expert in the family court for the length of time mentioned in the previous paragraph and have given evidence hundreds of times.

I am instead, a professionally qualified social worker, who has specialised in working with children and families within the court arena.

Now, you may have negative views about social workers. Many, or quite a high percentage of people, within the UK tend to hold negative views about social workers, and if this applies to you, I would ask you to try to suspend any negative views you may hold, so as to ensure that even if you do hold such views, that it does not prevent you from gaining the benefit of my many years of experience in this vital area.

Indeed, I would argue that it is precisely my position, as an expert regarding child care, safeguarding/child protection and in undertaking parenting assessments, that has placed me in a key position to provide you with the expertise you can take advantage of throughout this book.

I should perhaps point out (as I consider the point needs emphasising) that lawyers and barristers have great skill as mentioned earlier in firing questions at you, and at knowing the case before the court. However, they are not generally anywhere near as skilled, at giving evidence at court.

This is because it is not what they do. Simply stated, it is not a part of a lawyer's duties. The only time they give evidence on the witness stand, would be in connection with their own private matter(s) but it is not something they need to endure as part of their job.

So, whilst they have substantial experience in posing questions to you, they themselves are not accustomed to sitting in the witness box having questions fired at them. This means that although in some cases, lawyers may offer some advice and assistance around how you answer questions when in the box, they are not always best placed to support and prepare you for giving evidence.

Experts such as myself, on the other hand, regularly have to sit in the witness box for hours at a time, and it is these experiences over many years, which I consider more than qualifies me to write this book.

Let me ask you a question: “Who would you prefer to listen to and receive advice from, someone with years of experience of being in the position you will be in, and knows what it feels like?

Or someone who knows much about family law, but has rarely, if ever, been in your position - on the receiving end of being cross-examined at court?

My first few experiences within the family court were excruciatingly painful, bruising occurrences.

My very first experience at the family court (I no longer feel embarrassed or ashamed to share it with you) was an absolute ‘baptism of fire,’ which left me feeling inept, demoralised and highly traumatised.

At that time, I was a naïve, inexperienced social worker, who was in no way prepared for the atmosphere at court, the questions that were to be hurled at me, or the way I was left feeling, following the mauling I received from those who cross-examined me.

If you were to ask me now how and why I was able to go back into court after my first court appearance, I would not be able to offer you a coherent answer. I really don't know how I was able to. But as is so often the case in life, it was an experience such as that, which propelled me to learn the things I needed to learn, to defend myself against carnivorous legal wolves, who see you as nothing more than a piece of meat, to sink their razor sharp teeth into.

The gulf between who I was then, in terms of my ability to answer questions skilfully, and present my evidence in a cogent manner, and who I am now, is astounding, but it did not take me years to make this change. I began to learn something useful every time I went to court, and as a result I became very skilled very quickly.

It was a 'sink or swim' situation, and I was not prepared to go under again. I had done that and had the psychological and emotional scars to prove it. In essence, I simply made a choice to prevent myself from ever being savaged, in the witness box and from that time onwards I never have been.

Now, instead of feeling inept and being made to look like a fool, I have learned to answer questions in a manner, which not only allows me to leave the witness box feeling proud of my performance, but I also know from their body language, and the emotional energy I am receiving, that the person questioning me has not heard the answers they want to hear.

Which means they have less questions to ask you, because your answers are not helping their case; they are instead showing you up in a positive light, which often results in them having to discard a whole line of further questioning, because those questions are now inapplicable.

This is what I am now able to do on a consistent basis, when in the witness box, due to repeated experiences of giving evidence, and it is what you can also learn to do. There is absolutely no doubt in my mind, that you can quickly learn the skills required to competently give evidence at court.

You do not need to be super articulate or intelligent, you just need to want to learn and be willing to put the effort into doing it.

Now, let me answer some of the questions, which are probably forming in your mind:

Q. If I am already a nervous person, will it be impossible for me to learn this?

A. Absolutely not. You can learn this and become good at it, if you want to!

Q. Do I have to have any legal or social work training in order to do this?

A. No, you do not.

Q. What if I've got no qualifications at all?

A. As long as you can speak English, and string sentences together, you can do this!

Q. Am I going to have to devote some time, and attention to learning how to manage giving evidence?

A. Yes, of course you are. The more time you devote to it, the more skilled you will become.

Q. How long will it take to feel a level of confidence about giving evidence?

A. Well, that all depends on you, and what you put into it.

But let's face it, you are going to spend much time dreading attending court anyway, so you might as well do something positive with that time, which will reduce your fears and increase your confidence. Instead of spending time worrying about it, or 'burying your head in the sand,' you can spend that time learning how to answer questions and manage your fears, prior to and during your time in court.

It is vital that you learn to answer questions appropriately and learn to regulate your emotions, such that you present reasonably confidently.

When being cross-examined by someone who senses doubt and fear from you as a witness, you can be sure that they will become emboldened, almost in a similar way that an animal does when it smells blood or senses your fear. They become excited and prepare to go for the jugular vein.

In my experience, lawyers and barristers are the same, it's their job after all, and what they get paid for. The more anxious and diffident you sound or appear, the more voracious, lengthy and aggressive their questioning is likely to be.

So, the more confident you feel, the more confident you will present, and giving you the insights, understanding, tips and tactics to augment your confidence, is what this book is all about.

It is about offering you specialist, insider knowledge and providing you with the opportunities, to learn the skills you need to properly defend yourself whilst in the witness box.

What I would add to that is, if you do that well enough, you are not just defending yourself, you are providing the judge with information consistent with your case (whatever you have been arguing) and giving him or her, strong reasons to, not only believe you, but place a high value on what you are saying.

Your goal in giving evidence should always be, not just to defend yourself, but to provide the court with compelling arguments, which support your statements or case.

You are at court to get a favourable outcome, right?

You therefore want to persuade the judge to look favourably on the information you supply, and the way to do this is to give the judge convincing reasons to value and prefer your evidence over your opponent's, or other witnesses.

So, who is this book for and what benefits will you gain from reading it?

This book is primarily for you, if you are a parent who is separating or divorcing, involved in private law family disputes and cannot agree on the decisions you should make with regard to your children.

Private law cases relate to disputes between you and your former partner, or the other parent. They are private law matters because your local authority has **not** brought the matter to the court. The case has instead been initiated by yourself, or your ex-partner, and thus it is a private law matter.

This does not mean that the local authority cannot, or may not become involved in some way, but the crucial factor here is, that the case was either initiated by the other parent, or by you.

It will, I hope, be useful to you whether you are a litigant in person (you are representing yourself at court) or have instructed a solicitor to represent you.

The book is also applicable to you if you are a parent who is involved in **Public law** care proceedings. This refers to when a local authority makes an application to the court under section 31 of the Children Act 1989, where the local authority (the applicant) considers that your child is suffering significant harm, or is likely to suffer significant harm, and you (the respondent) are worried that you may lose your child.

It may also be of benefit to both newly qualified, and more experienced social workers, who are required to attend court, to provide evidence with regard to their case, or cases in public law care proceedings.

These are the three main groups of people who this book is written for.

Just to be clear with you, as I am not a legal professional, the book is written in a way as to hopefully, make sense to lay people, using as few legal terms and jargon as possible.

If you are a parent reading this book, in connection with your private law family case, or a parent involved in public law proceedings, I have below outlined the important information you need to know, about the legislation (Children Act) in order to provide evidence competently.

Please note that whenever I talk about the local authority instigating care proceedings, or applying to the court to initiate legal proceedings against you, or another parent, I am discussing public law proceedings.

I have included the basic concepts, which you need to have an understanding of. Obviously, if you are a social worker you will probably know more about the relevant legislation than parents generally do, and if not, you will likely have little problem in knowing where to acquire the information you need.

Legal Information For Parents

If you are anything like me, the thought of writing about or learning a lot of legal information, may not exactly thrill you or fill you with excitement. But I'd like to share a little story with you that I think exemplifies just how important it is for you to know the law, or that particular part of the law, relevant to you when it matters most.

This story occurred many years ago, whilst I was in the middle of training to become a social worker. As part of my training I had been placed in an advice centre, and the person who was my Practice Teacher (the person responsible for providing me with learning opportunities) was trained as a lawyer.

Anyway, one day whilst driving I approached a junction near Marble Arch in London, and just as I went through the lights, they changed from amber to red. Some few seconds later, I was stopped by a police officer, who told me that I was being charged for driving through traffic lights, whilst the lights were red.

As a result, I had to attend a court hearing. The penalties at the time of being found guilty of the offence, I think ranged from either losing my licence for a period of time, or having several points placed on my driving licence, and paying a fine that, at that moment in time, would have been very difficult for me to have paid.

Obviously I was quite worried about what the outcome would mean for me, and being very young at the time, I had never been to court for a driving, or any other type of offence. I chose to speak to my Practice Teacher about the incident and the fact that I was going to have to go to court to defend myself.

He listened to me quietly and when I had finished simply said: "When the prosecution brings a case to court, the onus is on them to prove **beyond a reasonable doubt** that you committed the offence."

I thanked him for the information, but being worried and inexperienced in such matters I didn't have a clue about how, or whether I would have a chance to use it at court.

On the day of the court hearing, I attended court, somewhere in Marylebone, central London, wearing a shirt and tie, and armed with that one sentence provided for me by my Practice Teacher.

There were at least between twenty to thirty other young men like myself, who all seemed to have been charged with the same or similar offence as me.

It occurred to me as we were herded into the court room, where we were all being called to give evidence, one after the other, that we were like a group of animals just waiting to be slaughtered.

One by one these young men, were giving their accounts of what had occurred to the court, and the outcomes were all the same. They were all being found guilty and at the very least, forced to pay, what were to these young men, hefty fines.

When my turn came to give my account, after the police officer had provided their evidence against me, I told the judge that it was a close matter, but that the lights changed from amber to red at the second I passed through them.

The judge then asked me if I had anything further to say before he passed judgement.

This was it, my moment of opportunity.

I looked at him and said: "I understand that when the prosecution brings a case such as this to court, that they have to prove beyond a reasonable doubt that the offence was committed..." I paused at that point, more out of fear and worry, than for effect. Then I continued: "...In this case, as I see it, it comes down to my word against the police officer's word...and I don't consider that as proof beyond a reasonable doubt."

The judge paused for just a moment before replying, a faint smile seemed to flicker across his features as he did so, and then he said words that I have never forgotten: "… I think... I am forced to agree with you."

I was euphoric – out of this world!

The rest of the young men all looked at me with complete astonishment. What the hell had just happened? It was to them a mystery – some form of magic that seemed incredible!

As I waltzed out of the court building that day, it felt like I was floating on air. Anyone would have thought I had won a million pounds from the expression on my face, but when I eventually came back down to earth, I thought about the fact that going through the lights on amber as it turned red, had been a close call.

Then I thought about the many other people, normal average people, just like you and me, who are judged to have broken the law when they may not have at all, but because they were not armed with the exact piece of legal knowledge that they needed to know, and apply at the appropriate time, they suffered some form of penalty as a result.

They were not able to defend themselves, simply because they did not know that in England and Wales for example, in criminal law cases, that the defendant – you or I, are presumed innocent, until the prosecution proves guilt beyond a reasonable doubt. To prove your guilt beyond a reasonable doubt, the prosecution would need to provide evidence or proof that leaves others sure of your guilt

Please bear in mind that at the time this happened to me, I wasn't even yet a social worker, I was just an ordinary person like you (and I still am) the only difference between me and all those other young guys, was that I dressed up for court and I had taken the time – well I was fortunate really - to have gained information, that made all the difference in court on the day.

Oh yes, I almost forgot!

Had I been really savvy at the time, I believe I could have asked the judge to award me some sort of compensation, in terms of paying my travel fees, but I was just too euphoric at the time to be able to think practically.

I shared that story with you because, despite the fact that the law is not something that tends to evoke excitement within me, knowing about relevant legislation is nevertheless, of crucial importance at certain times in your life.

If you're going to the family court, whether you are enthralled or bored stiff, by information about family law, this is definitely one of those certain times in your life, when you are going to need to know, about the law as it relates to your case.

The main legislation relating to your family law matter, is encompassed in the Children Act 1989 and subsequent revisions to the act.

The Children Act 1989 produced a number of main principles, terms and concepts that as a parent you need to have an understanding about.

The first and extremely important principle is that the **welfare of the child is of paramount consideration**. This then, is a most important consideration the courts use, to guide the decisions they make with regards to your child, and any other child they are concerned with.

They are assisted in looking at the welfare of your child by considering the Welfare Checklist. This represents the legal criteria the courts need to address when determining decisions that involve your child.

The Welfare Checklist consists of 7 criteria as follows:

1. The ascertainable wishes and feelings of your child.
2. Your child's physical, emotional and educational needs
3. The likely effect on your child of changes in circumstances
4. Your child's age, sex, background and any other characteristics which will be relevant to the court's decision

5. Any harm your child has suffered, or may be at risk of suffering
6. The capability of yourself and your child's other parents (or any other person the court finds relevant) of meeting your child's needs.
7. The range of powers available to the court under this Act in the proceedings in question.

Now, it is highly unlikely that you or any other parent, would disagree with, or deny that the welfare of your child is of paramount consideration. What you may consider as more debatable, is how the court comes to decide upon, or what they interpret as being in your child's welfare or best interests.

The Family courts consider that children are generally and wherever possible, **best brought up within their own families.**

Obviously, if the local authority has instigated public law care proceedings, they have concerns about your ability to keep your child safe, or meet their needs, and promote their overall wellbeing.

Since the local authority have instigated care proceedings, they are the applicants, and they have what is known as the '**burden of proof,**' in relation to proving their case.

Essentially then, the onus is on the local authority to prove that your child is suffering significant harm (or is beyond your parental control). The standard of proof required in family law cases, is that the applicant has to prove that on the **balance of probabilities,** their case is true.

This is different from criminal law, as mentioned earlier, where the prosecution has to prove a defendant's guilt **beyond a reasonable doubt**.

For the local authority to win their case, the court must be satisfied, given the evidence, that your child is more likely than not, to have suffered significant harm.

To put it another way, if the court decides that it is 50% likely that the applicant's case is true, then the local authority fails to win their case, as the responsibility rests with them to prove to a higher balance of probabilities i.e. 51% and above, that their case is true.

Clearly then, as I hope it is plain to you, there is a very fine difference between you winning and losing, via the balance of probabilities standard of proof.

Children should be protected, **if at risk of significant harm via the use of appropriate professional services, designed to safeguard and promote their wellbeing.** But professionals should not be interfering in the lives of families any more than is absolutely necessary, to keep them safe.

Parents with **Children In Need** should be helped to raise their children within their own home via the appropriate help, and working in partnership with services from local authorities, private and voluntary services.

The Children Act 1989 defines a child in need, as one who is unlikely to achieve or maintain, a reasonable level of health or development, or whose health and development is likely to be significantly or further impaired without the provision of services; or a child who is disabled.

When considering the welfare of children, the courts bear in mind that they should **avoid delay** as this is not considered to be in their best interests.

The **'No Order'** principle means that the court will only make an order if it considers that to do so, will be better than making no order.

The court considers it important that **the views and wishes of your child/ren should be ascertained,** and dependent upon your child's age, and level of understanding, they should be kept updated or advised about what is happening with regard to them.

The older your child is, the more weight is placed on his or her views and wishes. If your child is aged about 12 and above, it is considered he or she should have an increasingly important say in decisions that affect them.

The Children Act introduced the concept of **parental responsibility,** for or towards your children; which refers to the rights, duties, responsibilities and legal power you hold with regard to your child.

If you hold parental responsibility with regard to your child, whether you are living with your child, or not, you should be kept informed about him or her, and should be consulted with regard to decisions about your child's future.

Even if your child is in the care of the local authority, and they share parental responsibility with you, as occurs when your child is made the subject of a care order, or if your child is accommodated under section 20 of the Children Act, you still continue to hold parental responsibility, and thus should be consulted in connection with decisions relating to your child.

So, who has parental responsibility and how do you acquire it, if you do not have it?

If you are the birth mother for your child, you will hold parental responsibility unless your child has been adopted, which has the effect of severing your parental responsibility. Or a parental order has been made severing your parental responsibility, due to you being a surrogate mother.

You will hold parental responsibility if you are a father, and were married to the mother at the time of your child's birth, in which case you will both share parental responsibility for your child.

If you are not married but are the birth father of your child, who was born before the 1st December 2003, you will not have held parental responsibility, unless you acquired it in the following ways:

Via a court making a parental responsibility order.

By marrying the birth mother of the child.

By entering into a parental Responsibility agreement with your child's mother.

In the respect of married lesbian couples, or civil partners of mothers, if you were married to your same sex spouse, and your child was conceived via artificial insemination, both parents/partners will have parental responsibility.

If you were in a civil partnership and your child was conceived via artificial insemination on, or following the 6th April 2009, your civil partner will also have parental responsibility for your child.

If both of your names are placed on your child's birth certificate, your child will have no legal father.

Let us now turn to look at the **private law** orders that you need to be aware of. They come under what is called Section 8 Orders.

Since the Children and Families Act, 2014, four orders are now available under section 8 as detailed below:

Child Arrangement Orders (CAO) are orders that settle the arrangements concerning who your child will live with and spends time with. A CAO can be granted to more than one person irrespective of whether they live together or not.

You need to be aware that joint or shared CAO does not mean or imply that you and the other parent will both be receiving an equal amount of time with your child.

If you are granted a CAO you will have parental responsibility for your child until that order ceases (since CAO's confer parental responsibility) but if you are the parent with PR, prior to being granted a CAO, you will continue to have PR after the order ceases.

The main people who can apply for a Child Arrangement order without the permission of the court are parents, step-parents, special guardians and a legal guardian of your child (a legal guardian is someone who has the legal authority and duty to raise your child, in the event that you are not around to do so yourself).

However, there are a number of other situations in which people, other than the 4 named types of people mentioned above, can apply for Child Arrangement orders.

People can apply for a CAO under the following circumstances:

If you have lived with a child for at least three years within the last 5 years and you make an application to the court within 3 months of the child no longer living with you.

Where a CAO is in force and you (as the person who wishes to make the application) have the consent or support of the person the child is legally living with.

Similar to the circumstances in the previous point, if the child is in local authority care and the local authority provide their consent to you to make the application.

You can make the application to the court, provided that you have the consent of those who hold parental responsibility for the child concerned

As you can see grandparents do not have an automatic right to make an application for a Child Arrangement Order. They would need to meet the criteria named above, or failing that, apply to the court for leave to obtain a Child Arrangement order.

Child Arrangement Orders normally cease, when your child reaches the age of 16 but under exceptional circumstances, the order may continue until he or she is 18.

In the event that you and your ex-partner rekindle your relationship and recommence, or begin cohabiting, the order will cease to have effect 6 months after you begin or resume living together.

If you have been granted a CAO and you are the named person your child, lives or resides with, you will be able to take your child abroad for up to one month without the need for anyone else's approval.

Should you require a longer period abroad, you would then need the approval of anyone else with parental responsibility.

Alternatively you could achieve the same result by obtaining the court's approval, as a result of being granted a Specific Issue order.

If you are a non-resident parent, or a parent named in the CAO as the person your child spends time with, you will not be able to take your child on holiday abroad without the approval of the person your child resides with.

In the event that you are unable to obtain the approval of the parent your child lives with, your only alternative is to apply to the court, allowing as much time as possible prior to the dates you would like to take your child abroad.

The same principle applies, in the event that you wish to change your child's name. You will first require the consent of the other parent, or those with parental responsibility. If their consent is not forthcoming, your recourse is to seek the approval of the court, via obtaining a Specific Issue Order.

But what can you do if the other parent named on the CAO chooses not to comply with the order?

If this happens, it is open to anyone named in the order (irrespective of whether you are the parent the child lives with, or has contact with) to make an application to the court, to seek to ensure the order made is complied with.

You can then make an application to the family court. They will then list the case within 3 weeks, normally with the same judge who was in charge of the previous proceedings.

The court has sanctions it can impose on parents who fail to comply with orders made, and has at its disposal a number of powers to ensure the compliance of those named in the order.

A CAO now encompasses what used to be referred to as residence or contact orders, and if you have one of those previous orders there is no need for you to re-apply.

In the past you would apply for a Contact order if you sought contact with your child, or a Residence order for your child to reside with you. Now, a CAO when granted, resolves the details of the arrangements for both issues at the same time.

As well as dealing with who your child should live with, and/or who they should spend time with (bearing in mind that courts can make shared care arrangements) they can also address matters such as, whether your child's name should be changed or not, which school they should attend, and can decide issues related to whether your child should be administered medical treatment, or be brought up in a certain religious faith.

Child Arrangement Orders also encompass (as well as what were previously residence and contact orders) what is known as, **Specific Issue Orders** and **Prohibited Steps Orders.**

Specific Issue orders relate to specific issues of how your child is raised. For example, they apply to matters such as, where your child attends school, issues about whether it's in the best interests of your child's name being changed, or the religious faith and customs your child is exposed to.

The fourth type of CAO is a **Prohibitive Steps order**. This is an order designed to stop or prevent the other parent or guardian from taking a certain step or action. A Prohibitive Steps order can be used, for example, to stop your child coming into contact with the other parent's partner, if you consider they pose a risk to your child.

A **Contact Order** is an order which requires the resident parent, or the parent who your child resides with, to permit contact with you or someone else.

Now that you have hopefully, an understanding of the legislation, as going to court is a very stressful and confusing experience, it may be helpful to offer you as a parent in private law proceedings, an understanding of the court process, and the different hearings you may have to attend.

Since you are reading this book, I am assuming that you have attended a Mediation Information and Assessment Meeting (MIAM) but it was not successful in satisfactorily resolving your dispute with your ex-partner or other parent, and thus still need to know all you can about the court process, and presenting your evidence at court.

Mediation is an alternative method of attempting to resolve your dispute and your attendance at a mediation meeting is compulsory, prior to applying to the court for a CAO.

Mediation however, is not considered suitable in all family cases, and in cases where it is not considered suitable, mediators have to sign off the appropriate form, and explain the reason why it might be necessary, for you to receive an exemption from mediation.

Cases where there have been incidents of violence, and/or domestic abuse are a good example of when a mediator may consider a mediation meeting inappropriate.

Following the making of an application to the family court, you as the applicant (the person who made the application) or you as the respondent (the person responding to the application) will be asked to attend a hearing, referred to as the **First Hearing Dispute Resolution Appointment** (commonly abbreviated to **FHDRA**).

The FHDRA is a very important hearing and it is vital that you take the time to ensure you do not miss out any information or evidence that is essential to your case. It will cause delay if you attempt to bring up salient matters later, and it could result in seriously jeopardising your case.

The purpose of this hearing is to help the court understand, as clearly as possible what the issues are which are in dispute, between the parties (in other words between you and the other parent) in order to discover whether there is any possibility, for you and your ex-partner to arrive at a consensus.

It will be helpful for you to spend some time prior to the first hearing, clarifying what it is you want, and what you propose should happen, since the court will want to know what your proposals are and the reasons for them.

You may find it helpful to write a position statement, documenting a brief summary of your case, and what you want the court to consider, prior to attending court. You should send a copy of your position statement, to the other party as well as to the court.

At the FHDRA, a CAFCASS officer should be present. Before the hearing, the CAFCASS Officer, should have undertaken background checks with the police and the local authority, on the parties to ensure there are no safeguarding risks or welfare issues for the children that the court needs to be aware of.

These checks also involve a telephone interview with you and the other party to discover if you have any concerns regarding the welfare and safety of your child.

CAFCASS then undertakes to provide this safeguarding letter, at least three days prior to your first hearing.

CAFCASS is an abbreviation for the Children and Family Court Advisory and Support Service. It was established to promote the wellbeing of children and families in family court cases in England.

CAFCASS Cymru is an organisation in the Welsh Government that provides a voice for any child in Wales, involved with the Family Justice system.

The safety checks undertaken by CAFCASS, are also known as a Schedule 2 letter, and this is shared with both parties. The only reason this would not be shared openly with both parties, is if it was considered that doing so would place the children or either party at risk, or the document would expose sensitive information which the other party was not aware of.

In the event that the parties are unable to come to an agreed solution, the court will seek to identify the areas of disagreement and the reasons why they are unable to reach a consensus.

The role of the court will be to focus on whatever evidence will be needed to help the court at a later hearing, determine what is in your child's best interests.

If there are concerns about the welfare of your child for any reason, the court may request that the CAFCASS Officer writes a section 7 report, centred on the welfare of your child, to assist the court to make appropriate safe decisions.

If the dispute between the parties relates to contact or residence orders and a party makes allegations of a serious nature, in such circumstances the judge may decide to suspend contact whilst investigations are carried out.

Or it might be decided, that contact takes place at a supervised venue or contact centre, whilst matters pertaining to the allegations are investigated.

Fact Finding Hearings are hearings convened specifically to determine from the evidence whether an alleged occurrence did or did not occur. In order to arrive at a decision concerning the allegation, you and the other party are asked to give evidence, which generally includes being cross-examined.

Following hearing all of the evidence, the judge will come to a decision about whether the allegation happened, or did not.

Final hearings are hearings in which the judge takes into account all the evidence before the court. This includes all the written and oral evidence by yourself and the other party, any reports by CAFCASS and the local authority. If there was a Fact Finding Hearing, the judge will consider this evidence, and any finding made during that hearing.

The judge then, having collated and assessed all the evidence before the courts, will, with the aid of the 'welfare checklist,' determine what is in the best interests of your child.

In coming to his or her decision concerning your child, the judge will give consideration to the 'no order' principle, or may decide to make a Child Arrangement order, setting out details about residence and contact arrangements with regard to your child.

A Review Hearing may be set during the court proceedings, or at the time a final hearing is set. The purpose of the review hearing is to review the case.

The setting of a review hearing during the life of the proceedings, is normally to act as a mechanism to enable the court to maintain control of the case, ensuring that the evidence timetable is adhered to and, for example that any interim contact ordered, is proceeding as directed.

After the making of a final order there is a provision which makes it possible to allow the court to leave the case open for some months and set a date for a future review hearing.

A review hearing which can be vacated if the parties agree it is not necessary, is a hearing designed to ensure compliance with the final order. These orders, which are not frequently used may be useful, particularly when one of the parties exhibits hostility and there is a concern that the contact arrangements may not be complied with.

Under such circumstances it might be prudent to request that the judge leave the case open and place a clause in the order giving you permission to return to court within a matter of months. Thus ensuring that if the other party refuses to adhere to the order, within the time period, the matter can be restored to court without the need for you to pay a further court fee and for the court to address the matter of non- compliance.

Now let us turn to look at the important concepts, and information you will need an understanding of, if you are a parent in public law care proceedings.

If you are a parent involved in public law care proceedings, you will be eligible to receive legal aid, and thus will be legally represented.

The circumstances under which your child/ren, may become subject to care proceedings, occur in the event that Children's Services of the local authority, in which you live, consider that your child may be suffering **significant harm,** and as a result, may apply to the court for permission to intervene, to protect your child.

It is not easy to describe precisely, what is meant by the concept of significant harm, but it is defined in the Children Act 1989 as follows:

Harm means ill-treatment, or impairment of health and development. Ill-treatment includes sexual abuse, and forms of ill-treatment which are not physical, thus including emotional abuse.

Impairment of health and development, for instance, can include the impairment resulting from being exposed to, the ill-treatment of another. Physical abuse is not explicitly included, but is an obvious form of harm.

Health includes both physical and mental health. Development includes physical, intellectual, emotional, social and behavioural development.

In order to determine whether the health or development of your child is being significantly impaired, the act instructs that we compare the health and development of your child with that which could be reasonably expected of a similar child.

Significant refers to the level of harm, being sufficiently serious enough, so as to warrant the intervention of the local authority.

In order for the local authority to gain a care order or a supervision order, with regard to your child, the **threshold criteria** has to be met. In other words, the local authority (applicants) must prove that your child is suffering, or is likely to suffer, significant harm and the harm, or likelihood of harm, is attributable to either:

The care given to your child, or likely to be given to him or her, if the order were not made, not being what it would be reasonable to expect a parent to give, or

Your child being beyond parental control.

So, let's suppose that you as a parent, are at the stage where the Children's Services of your local authority believe that the threshold criteria are met in connection with your child.

Prior to a decision being made, to instigate care or supervision proceedings, a legal planning meeting needs to be convened. This is not a meeting you will be asked to attend, or have any input in, or will even be aware of at the time.

A key purpose of the legal planning meeting is to decide, whether it is considered the threshold criteria has been met, and if so, determine the following:

a) If it is in your child's best interests to provide a further period of support for the family in an effort to avoid court proceedings, or.

b) Whether court proceedings should be commenced immediately.

If the latter decision is reached, then your local authority will send you, or those with parental responsibility, one of two following letters, as follows:

1. A letter before proceedings informing you that court proceedings are being considered; or

2. A letter of issue stating that court proceedings are being instigated.

If you are yet to give birth, the timing of you being sent either of these letters is critical, and should take into account the risk of an early birth. Given this risk and time permitting, a letter should hopefully be dispatched to you at, or prior to, 24 weeks gestation.

The letter before proceedings should contain the following:

a) What the concerns of the local authority are.

b) An account of the support that has already been provided to you

c) Clarity about what you need to do and by when, as well as what support will be provided for you, to prevent proceedings being initiated.

d) Providing information about how and where to gain legal advice, and representation and the importance of doing so for your case.

It should contain your invitation, along with anyone else who has parental responsibility, to a Pre-Proceedings Meeting, otherwise known as a Public Law Outline Meeting (PLO) and the date of the meeting must occur within 7 days of its receipt.

The PLO meeting, unlike the legal planning meeting is a meeting where your attendance is required, indeed it is vital. Those in attendance will include a local authority solicitor, your child's social worker, yourself and your legal representative or solicitor and anyone else who has parental responsibility for your child.

In the event that you are not on good terms with the other parent, or are not comfortable in their presence, you can tell the social worker who may then attempt to arrange separate PLO meetings.

The purpose of the meeting, is to attempt to come to an agreement concerning the safety and wellbeing of your child, without it being necessary to issue court proceedings.

It is important for you to recognise that the PLO meeting is yours, and the local authority's last opportunity to avoid court proceedings.In the event that the local authority sends you a letter, inviting you to a PLO meeting, if you have not taken the matter seriously before, this is the time for you to 'wake up' and act!

This is definitely not the time to stick your head in the sand. It is the time to move into action, and fast!

Essentially during the meeting, the local authority will tell you what they want you to do and often will ask you to sign a written agreement which includes all the things they want you to do, which they consider will both keep your child safe, meet his or her welfare needs, and avert the need for court proceedings.

Your legal representative will advise you concerning whether you should sign it or not, informing you if there is anything in the agreement which is unjustified. They will also advise you of the consequences in the event you choose not to sign the agreement.

After the meeting, if you have been able to do all that was requested of you, and within the time period, the PLO process could come to an end.

If, however, concerns persist, it may be that another PLO meeting is convened, or a decision might be taken that the concerns are sufficiently serious, that they immediately instigate court proceedings. Under such circumstances, you are advised to contact a solicitor immediately.

If the local authority initiates care and supervision proceedings, under the revision brought in by the Children and Families Act 2014, there is a strong emphasis on completing the case without delay and strictly within a twenty-six week time period, commencing on the day the application was filed.

Your case is then expected to be completed within this time period, unless there are exceptional circumstances which make this not possible.

In the event that the local authority instigates care proceedings involving your child, there are a number of hearings that you will need to have some general understanding about.

A **Case Management Hearing** is a hearing where the court makes directions setting out how the case will proceed. It will address itself to matters such as defining what the key issues are; deciding upon the evidence required to enable the court to resolve the main issues and discerning whether there is any issue about the threshold which needs resolution.

Case Management hearings are normally brief hearings concerned with matters of procedure, so as to prepare the case for a hearing where final decisions can be made.

Issues Resolutions Hearings (IRH) are hearings set or directed to ascertain whether the care proceedings can be concluded early, and where this is not possible, the aim is to pinpoint and narrow down the issues for determination at the final hearing.

If the parties are in general agreement, then the Issue Resolution Hearing will then become treated as a final hearing.

At an IRH the court will clarify the main issues to be determined and the degree to which the issues can be narrowed or resolved. It resolves and/or narrows the issues by hearing evidence, and decides on the evidence to be heard, on the matters that remain to be resolved at the final hearing.

It will issue the final case management directions.

In the event that you or those with parental responsibility, and the social worker are unable to come to a consensus regarding your child, the case will continue on to a final hearing.

At the **Final Hearing** the court will decide whether a care order or supervision order is necessary to be made, in order to safeguard and meet the needs of your child. Remember that it has to consider the no order principle, i.e. whether making an order is better for your child than making no order at all.

If the court considers that an order needs to be made, final determinations will also be made concerning who your child lives with, what the contact details will be for parents and extended family members.

The range of possible final orders that the court can make are as follows:

A **Care Order** means that the local authority has been granted parental responsibility with regards to the care of your child. Effectively then, the local authority will share parental responsibility (PR) with you, but they have the overriding PR and will decide the details of your child's day to day care, so as to ensure their safety and wellbeing. They can decide matters such as where and with whom your child lives with.

Unless your child is discharged from the care order prior to the age of 18, they will remain **in care** or **looked after,** until reaching that age.

Although an **Interim Care order** (ICO) is not a final order, it is useful for you to know that during the proceedings, the court can make a temporary order placing your child under the local authority's care. This is referred to as an interim care order, since it is not a final order.

Interim care orders are made when the court considers there are reasonable grounds to believe the threshold criteria has been met.

Interim Care orders are subject to renewal. On the first renewal they can last for 8 weeks. Subsequent renewals occur every 4 weeks.

The implication for you of the court granting the local authority an interim care order is that they will then share parental responsibility with you, but will be able to make the decisions which they consider will safeguard your child's wellbeing.

As mentioned above, the local authority will have the legal power under a Care order, or an interim care order, to decide where your child lives and who they have contact with. They can decide to place your child with foster carers, family members or friends of your family. They can even place your child in your care, but this is unusual and would only likely occur under certain situations in which plans were put in place, to secure your child's safety and wellbeing.

You need to be aware that the local authority has a duty to provide parents (those with parental responsibility, family members and those who your child is emotionally attached to) with what is termed, a reasonable level of contact.

What is considered reasonable by the court will depend on factors such as whether your child is subject to an interim or a full care order; the age and level of understanding of a child and where the child lives; in other words the practical arrangements, involved in managing contact (particularly if your child is placed a long way from your home) and the care plan for your child.

In the event your child is made the subject of a care order, the social worker will have produced a **care plan,** which addresses all aspects of your child's life and is a plan to ensure they are kept safe and that their emotional, health, educational and developmental needs, are met throughout their childhood.

During court proceedings your child may be subject to an interim care order, and let's say for example, that the social worker has decided that contact can take place three times per week and that your contact should be supervised and occur within a contact centre.

This means that your contact will be observed by a contact supervisor whose role at yours and your child's contact, is both to ensure your child's safety and make a written account or report of your contact session. This written account is sent to the local authority's legal department and can be sent to your solicitor as these contact reports are often used as evidence in court proceedings.

Whilst you may be having contact, three times per week whilst your child is subject to an interim care order, in the event that the court makes a full care order (as opposed to an interim one) the implications concerning contact with your child may well have now changed markedly.

Your child is now subject to a care order and when the court makes a care order, it endorses your child's final care plan made by the social worker.

So whatever the care plan is for your child, in terms of how their long term plans are to be met (which could include placement with a family member or friend, long term foster care, Special Guardianship or adoption) the contact you receive will be consistent with the care plan.

If the care plan for your child is that of adoption, then your contact will eventually be reduced from three times per week to once per year, or more likely to indirect letterbox contact, of once or twice per year (normally on or around your child's birthday and around the Christmas period).

Although it may be obvious to you, but just so as to be clear, indirect or letterbox contact means that the only contact you will have with your child is via letters and pictures.

If the care plan is that of long term foster care, it may be that you will be able to receive contact more frequently, such as 6 times per year or monthly. But as I am sure you can appreciate only too well, the stakes as regards your contact and involvement in your child's life are monumental.

Another option open to the court during court proceedings is to make a **Supervision order.** If a supervision order is made, the local authority have a duty to advise, assist and befriend your child.

The difference between a supervision order and a care order is that the former order does not confer on the local authority parental responsibility in connection with your child. It is an order that is primarily used to safeguard or promote your child's wellbeing and oversee any progress made whilst your child remains living in your care, with a family member, or a Special Guardian.

A supervision order is made when the concerns, although serious, are not so serious as to warrant the making of a care order. Supervision orders are also made when your child is old enough to make their own decisions, and are unlikely or unwilling to be placed in care. They thus may be made the subject of a supervision order, in an effort to protect and safeguard them as much as possible.

Supervision orders can last for 12 months and can be extended on a yearly basis to a total of three years.

Just as the court can make an interim care order, it can also make an interim supervision order. The implication of an interim supervision order will be to place your child on a temporary basis, under the supervision of the local authority, pending the court's final decision about what is best for your child.

The court may make an interim supervision order where it considers it has reasonable grounds to believe that the threshold criteria has been met.

Supervision orders are sometimes made in conjunction with Special Guardianship orders.

A **Special Guardianship order** (SGO) is made when the court places your child, to live on a long term basis, with someone who is not your child's parent. A Special Guardian can be anybody over the age of 18, who has a relationship with your child, and has successfully been assessed by a social worker as being able to meet your child's long term care needs.

Special Guardians can apply on their own or can apply jointly with their spouse, partner or a family member. The person or persons, with whom your child would live with and be cared for, would be referred to as the Special Guardian/s for your child. It is a huge undertaking and anyone who assumes the role of a Special Guardian, assumes a great deal of responsibility throughout your child's childhood, until the age of 18.

The implication for you if your child is made subject to a Special Guardianship order is similar to that of a care order, in that the Special Guardian/s is granted parental responsibility. They then share PR with you, but have the overriding PR, as they are responsible for meeting your child's day to day needs and ensuring their safety, and that all their long term needs are met.

A Special Guardian order is a stronger order than a Child Arrangement Order, but a weaker order than an adoption order.

If you wish to apply to discharge a Special Guardian order before your child becomes 18, you need the permission of the court. You would need to demonstrate that there has been a significant change in your circumstances since the making of the SGO that warrants the court to look again at the matter.

Special Guardianship orders were introduced in the Adoption and Children Act law in 2002. Special Guardians should not be confused with Children's Guardians.

Children's Guardians (often just referred to in the family court as the Guardian) are social work trained professionals, who are skilled and experienced at working with children and families. They are appointed by the family court when the local authority initiates court proceedings to represent and advocate for the rights and interests of children.

Children's Guardian's work with solicitors, either appointed by themselves, or the court, to represent the interests of your child.

Children's Guardians are independent of the local authority, the court and any of the other parties. They work for CAFCASS either on an employed, or self-employed basis. Their role is a vital one for your child and yourself since they scrutinise the work of the local authority, or social worker, which includes reading the local authority files, seeing your child, yourself and ultimately writing an analysis of what they think is in the best interests of your child.

It is important that you realise, not only that the Children's Guardian does not just 'rubber stamp' whatever the social worker recommends, and makes their own recommendations, but also, that the court nearly always places a lot of weight on their recommendations.

Placement Orders

Were you aware that once the local authority has been granted a full care order in respect of your child, and your child is looked after, that the court can make an order which authorises them to place your child for adoption with any of the pool of adopters identified as appropriate by the local authority?

The court can make this order, whether you or the other parent are in agreement with it, and it lasts until an adoption order is made, or until the court makes a decision to end the order.

The effect of this order for you is that parental responsibility would now be shared between you, the local authority, and the proposed or future adopters of your child, once your child is placed with them.

As with the making of a care order, these are very serious steps with severe consequences for you, and for your child.

However, this will only happen following detailed assessments of your care and the risk to your child; an assessment of your ability to accept support, make use of it, and make the required changes, within what the court considers as your child's timescales.

The court will look at all the information and they will consider whether they require any further assessments. But if they agree with the local authority (after considering all the evidence that you and any other extended family members are unable to meet your child's needs, within the set timescale and that your child's current and long term needs are best secured via adoption) then the court will make a placement order.

You and other members of the family can contest the application of a placement order and you will be eligible to receive legal aid. A Children's guardian and solicitor for your child will be appointed, as in the case in application for care orders.

In the event of a placement order being made, you would need to show that there has been a significant alteration in your circumstances in order to be permitted to contest an application for an adoption order

It is important that you are made aware that although many parents make an application for leave to contest an adoption order application, their application is very rarely granted.

Even if you are successful in being granted leave to oppose an application to adopt, there are only a very small minority of cases within the country which have been successful.

Adoption Orders

An adoption order can be made with either yours and/or the other birth parent's consent, or by the court dispensing with yours and the other birth parent's consent.

This order has the effect of cutting the legal connection between you and your birth child. The adoptive parent or carer then becomes your child's legal parent, not just until they are 18, as in the case of a Special Guardianship order, but for the rest of your child's life.

You and your child's other parent, will of course continue to be your child's biological parents, but your legal powers and duties will cease once your child becomes adopted.

Now that you have a clearer understanding about the private and public law legislation, the orders and the process your family law matter will likely take, let's turn your attention to focus on parenting, or the care you provide for your child.

Key Learning Points

- It is important to have an understanding of the law applicable to your situation or circumstance.
- It is helpful to have an understanding of the terminology used by lawyers and the family court.
- It is very useful to have some knowledge about the different orders used in the family court.
- It is also useful to have an understanding of the family court process and the length of time involved in bringing the case to a conclusion.
- The information supplied above is by no means exhaustive and parents seeking more information can obtain more information online and from other sources such as Citizen Advice Bureau and other useful agencies and resources.

Parenting

"To be a good father and mother requires that parents defer many of their own needs and desires in favour of the needs of their children. As a consequence of this sacrifice, conscientious parents develop a nobility of character and learn to put into practice the selfless truths taught by the Saviour himself."

James E. Faust

"Every word, facial expression, gesture, or action on the part of a parent gives the child some message about self-worth. It is sad that so many parents don't realise what messages they are sending."

Virginia Satir

Whilst planning how to write this book, it occurred to me that you can't really be expected to give a good account of yourself, in respect of the written and verbal evidence you provide at the family court, unless you have a good understanding of the type of care your child needs in order to be kept safe and to develop appropriately.

Now, what I have learned, from working with hundreds of parents in over thirty years, is that as a parent of your child, you will tend to believe that you know what is best for them because they are your child.

In other words, you might say, as many parents often do: “she’s my child, so I know what’s best for her.”

I guess every parent understands that kind of gut, emotional response.

What you are really saying, when making such a statement, is that she is your child and this implies that you love her more than anyone else, and thus that you are best positioned to know what is best for her.

Of course you love her and the statement you are making may be absolutely true. However, there is no guarantee at all that because you love your child, that you automatically know what’s best for them.

I am sure I am likely to upset a few people here, but just because you gave birth to your child, or fathered her and love her, it does not necessarily follow that you know what is best for her or are able to put her needs first.

Even if you may know what’s best for your child. It does not necessarily follow that you are able, or best placed to provide the type of care that secures your child’s best interests.

Your response to this might be to assert that there is equally no guarantee that Cafcass Officers, social workers or the court, always know what is best for your child either.

In my view, you would be correct to say so. But the reality is that the court is now involved in your case and as a result, in order for you to obtain the best result for your child, you are going to have to become very familiar with what the court views as good or appropriate parenting.

One of the problems I think you as a parent face (and again, when I say you I mean, you, me, or parents generally) is that you have, in some way, learned to see your child as your property.

The language you use in connection with your children denotes the way you think, although I think it is rare that parents take the time to consider or recognise this.

You might disagree with me concerning this point, but what I am trying to say is, if you see yourself as being responsible for your child and them having their own discrete needs, wishes and feelings, you are then in a better position to separate their needs from those of your own.

Sometimes parents, especially at times of stress and hardship, overlook this and tend to see things from their own point of view, assuming incorrectly, that what's best for them is one and the same as what's best for your child.

As a parent you have to be able to be aware of and distinguish between your needs and those of your child's.

They are not the same.

Your child's needs will be different from yours because your child is at a different stage and level of development from you. He or she is also unique and will have their own distinct personality, wants and needs, which will change over time as they grow, develop and become more independent.

Recognising that your child has needs distinct from those of your own is one thing, but to act as a good or appropriate parent, you also have to be able to see things from your child's point of view, and have the capacity to prioritise your child's needs over those of your own or anyone else's.

If you are well attuned to your child's thoughts, wishes and feelings, you demonstrate what is known as empathy. Empathy is an essential ability in parenting and indeed in any relationship, because it is necessary to be able to see things from your child's and other people's perspectives.

If you are unable to see things, from your child's point of view, you are in a position to cause your child a lot of harm, because your actions will not take account of their wishes and feelings.

Offering your child good or appropriate care entails not only considering your child's needs, but being able to prioritise them.

Essentially, this involves the notion of sacrifice – of placing your needs and wants behind those of your child's. It is this idea of sacrifice, or of subordinating your needs to those of your child's, that parents often struggle to do on a continuous or consistent basis.

Your capacity to forgo your own desires and provide and value whatever your child needs, over and above whatever your wants are, is a key indicator of appropriate parenting.

I urge you now and definitely throughout your family court case, to evaluate your attitudes, behaviour and decisions on this key criterion. This is, I strongly suggest, a vital exercise for you to do all the time.

You may be inclined to dismiss this suggestion, believing instinctively, that you already do this. But I would encourage you, to keep thinking about whether (and to what extent) your thoughts, decisions and actions, at their core, are consistently focused on what is in your child's best interests.

If you persevere with this exercise, you are likely to discover that much of what you consider to be in your child's interests is either debatably so, or at least not consistently so.

This is essential information for you, to discover now because it is this type of information that anyone cross-examining you will seek to exploit at your detriment.

Make no mistake, what I am suggesting that you do, is an exercise that will take up a lot of your time and thought. But it is well worth doing, and on a consistent basis, primarily because it is key to you gaining the insight you will need to demonstrate throughout your court case.

Even more importantly however, your ability to place your child's needs before your own and to see things from his or her point of view, will pay massive benefits in terms of your current and long term relationship with your child throughout your entire lives together.

Children have a wide variety of needs but invariably what your child wants, needs and values the most, especially when they are young, is for you to shower attention on them and give them quality time.

Giving your child your attention and spending quality time with them, being interested in them and their wants and feelings and praising them, are some of the most important things you can do for your child.

Often you might believe that what your child wants is the latest toy or expensive sports gear, but what is infinitely more valuable to your child and what he or she needs most, is the time, attention, love and praise you offer them.

Why?

Because they love you, and have a very strong need, which is to know you love them.

When you spend quality time with your children, it demonstrates to them that they are loved and worthy of your time and attention. This helps your child to feel valued, to develop a positive self-image, which supports the development of a healthy sense of self-esteem and positive mental health.

You should never be surprised about their awareness of your shortcomings in the following areas:

When you do not spend quality time with them – time focused completely on them.

When you are not emotionally available to them, because your interest is elsewhere, or are irritable when forced to give your child attention.

When you are inclined to criticise them, rather than praise their behaviour or efforts.

Neither should you be unaware of the detrimental impact your actions have on their self-image and sense of wellbeing.

Your child will know, because they will feel your absence (even when you are in the same room with them) or lack of emotional warmth towards them, and do not be surprised also if others such as your ex-partner, are also acutely aware of this.

Demonstrating your ability to listen to and understand your child's needs and place their needs in front of those of your own, is something you will have to show at court. It is vital that you do so in your everyday involvement with your child during and after your court case has come to an end if you are to develop and maintain a healthy long-term relationship with your child.

This applies whether your child resides with you or spends time with you at contact.

Now just so you know where I am coming from, I am not here to undermine or rubbish your strongly held views about what you consider is best for your child.

It may be that your parenting skills are highly developed and that everything you do is wholly consistent with what is in your child's best interests.

I do not know and have no way of knowing. I am not here to pass any judgement on your parenting, since I do not know you personally.

What my intention is, in talking with you about parenting skills, is simply to provide you with an understanding of the way the courts and professionals view or value what good or appropriate parenting is.

If I failed to do this and your parenting values and skills turn out to be very much in conflict with those of the courts, social workers, CAFCASS Officers, or other professionals (who the court are influenced by) then your chances of being seen as providing convincing evidence will be substantially reduced and the impact on your case will not be positive.

Consequently, it is necessary then for me to provide you with clear information about what professionals and the court view or value as both harmful parenting, and that which is considered consistent with promoting your child's health and wellbeing.

The parenting values and examples I mention below, are of course not an exhaustive list, but I hope and expect it provides you with as clear an understanding as possible.

In the event that you disagree with the parenting values described below, I would advise you, before discarding them to do three things:

Suspend your disbelief and try to maintain an open mind

Undertake your own extensive research (do not just look for information which supports your view)

Accept that whether you believe it or not, these are some of fundamental beliefs and values that the court will be guided by.

I think you should consider one other matter in addition to the three things noted above, and that is that, if you strongly disagree with the veracity of the values below, then it is highly likely that this will be observed in your evidence and used against you by those cross-examining you.

(Note that within public law cases you can be cross-examined by the other parties' advocates or lawyers, whereas in private law, it is normally only the lawyer for your ex-partner).

Beginning with your child's physical needs, he or she needs to live in a clean, ordered home environment. This does not mean that your house, needs to be spotless, perfectly hygienic and meticulously tidy.

It is unrealistic to expect you, or anyone else to constantly aspire to a perfectly hygienic, well-organised home. You, like everyone else, are allowed to experience periods when you are up and periods when you are down.

However, if it becomes evident that your home is frequently or continually in a messy, dirty and/or chaotic state, it has reached the point where concern is likely to be expressed in relation to your ability, to meet your child's physical care needs.

You, myself and everyone else would no doubt agree that every child needs an acceptable standard of hygiene. They need suitable beds, clean linen and clothes, an appropriate amount of clothes suitable for the weather conditions, as well as appropriate routines which ensure they receive regular amounts of fresh fruits, a healthy diet and regular meal times.

Children need routines with regard to regular bath times, oral hygiene and appropriate bed times to ensure they receive sufficient sleep every night, so that they can get up in time to get to school punctually and get the best out of their education. In addition, they require various types of stimulation, encouragement, praise and exercise.

Your child also needs to grow up in a home or environment which is free from physical violence and domestic abuse. Children need to feel safe, experience security, predictability, clarity and stability.

What do I mean by this?

I mean that your child needs to experience regular routines so that he knows with certainty what is likely to happen next (he knows when meal and bath times are, and who is caring for him, for example) and is able to benefit from living in a stable, secure home environment, rather than moving around frequently from one home environment to another, being exposed to different carers and being unable to gain a sense of belonging to a home environment, school and community.

Whilst the above statements pertaining to your child's physical care may be for the most part agreeable to you and other parents, where it becomes problematic is that parent's ideas about, for example, what a clean, safe, tidy and suitable home environment are, differ widely, depending on matters such as your own upbringing, mental health, stress levels and what you have become used to.

It is for reasons such as this, why parents (former partners) or a parent and a local authority, may come to very different conclusions about the standard of physical and emotional care your child is receiving.

In my experience, the capacity for disagreement is huge, since as human beings we can all see things very differently, depending on a variety of issues such as your experiences and backgrounds.

Take for example, the issue of discipline. If you are raising your child in a way (or with a parenting style) where you consider that it is wrong to physically chastise them, but choose to offer him/her no guidance, or instil no boundaries concerning what he/she is and is not allowed to do, then the care that you are offering is likely to be seen as equally concerning as a parent who believes in physically beating their child in order to ensure compliance with boundaries or rules.

Appropriate parenting regarding discipline, or any other parental matter, involves finding a suitable balance. It involves showing loving care, guidance and judgement - being willing to engage in a weighing-up process, in an effort to ensure decisions reached are in your child's best interests.

Too much instruction and discipline imposed without warmth and care can warp or damage your child. Just as a lack of boundaries or discipline, provided with an insufficient focus on your child's wellbeing, can result in your child harming themselves or others.

A delicate balance always need to be arrived at or negotiated with your child, especially as they grow older. This process of deliberation and negotiation is time consuming but essential in helping to ensure you make sound parenting decisions. It also shows your child that they are worthy of the time and effort you put into deliberating concerning decisions you make with them.

In terms of your child's emotional needs, this is an area where, in my view, parents may tend to struggle more in meeting their child's emotional needs than compared with meeting their physical needs.

When your child is a young baby, for him or her to begin to develop appropriately, they will need to be well attached, or to bond with, one or both of their parents or caregivers.

It is not enough to just meet your baby's physical needs (feeding, changing nappies, ensuring they are bathed and receive sufficient sleep). You have to also meet their emotional needs for love, attention, praise, affection, discipline and stimulation.

Babies and children generally have a huge capacity and need to receive love, attention and affection. Long before they start walking and following you around, they will follow you around with their eyes and show their excitement at being in your company by smiling, chuckling and kicking their legs in the air whilst maintaining eye contact with you.

In fact, it's important that you realise that, right from the very earliest beginning of your child's life, they are extremely vulnerable and totally dependent on your care.

That statement no doubt sounds a very obvious one, but you may be surprised to note that studies have been undertaken which indicate that your baby can be harmed by being exposed to domestic abuse whilst in the womb.

As a parent, you may believe that any arguments or conflict your child is exposed to when, he or she is a baby or very young, will not affect them because of their young age.

What I suggest to you is, if these are the thoughts you believe, the opposite is more likely to be true. The younger they are, the more dependent and vulnerable they are, and certainly the more frequently they witness abusive behaviour and conflict, the more harm they are exposed to. The more often, over the years of their childhood they witness, hear and experience such events, the more such incidents will seem natural and normal to them.

I also want you to recognise that parents often cling to the belief that their domestic disturbances are not overheard or witnessed by their child. Very often this is incorrect and your child knows, or is very aware, of the existence of the conflict.

So it's essential that you wake up to the fact, that your child watches and hears you when you may not be aware of it. Just because you are not aware of it, do not fall into the trap of thinking that your child is not conscious of what's going on, even if they are not able or willing to articulate it.

It's safe to say, that if degrees and higher qualifications, were being awarded to children in connection with their knowledge of their parents, your children would invariably graduate with first class honours degrees, because they watch you constantly, they are 'sponges' in that they absorb the information you provide and learn everything from you.

To your children you are real super heroes and there is a time in their life, often during your child's formative, years (0-7) and sometimes when much older than seven, when they have such faith in you, that they believe you can do anything.

This is a wonderful time and opportunity for you as a parent because you can establish a most amazing strong relationship with your child, if you know what you're doing.

Sadly, so many parents, due to a lack of awareness, and because of the everyday pressures and stresses of life, do not realise the gaping opportunity open to them at a crucial time in your child's childhood.

When you give your child the love, attention, affection, praise and encouragement that they require consistently from you, at the appropriate times, it is like seeing a flower blossom into full bloom before your very own eyes.

Your child is so full of love, beauty and wonder, they are loyal and passionate about you. They look up to you and want to do everything to please you during this phase of their life and sometimes for a long time afterwards.

When you fail to meet their emotional needs by neglecting to give them the love, attention, affection, encouragement and stimulation they require, they receive a message from you which they interpret as them not being worthy of your time, attention, love etc.

When this happens frequently enough, they eventually stop looking for this from you, but because you represent their world, they stop looking for this from other people also, because they have become used to being denied what they need most.

Often your children, when exposed to such parenting, become depressed and display flat emotions and a poor self-image.

It is absolutely vital to you, your court case and your child, that you recognise this, in the event that this scenario applies to you and your child. The difficulty for you as a parent hinges on the reality that your own insight and level of awareness very much depends on the parenting you received when you yourself were a young child.

However,if you keep a close eye on your child and remain open to the possibility that your child may well require you to be more emotionally available to them and conscious of just how incredibly sensitive your child generally is to you, you will not go too far wrong.

Your baby or young child, is a highly sensitive being, not only to you, and it is definitely in your interests, to keep that thought uppermost in your mind.

Your baby or young child may cry when they see another child crying and can be emotionally affected and harmed when they see another person being hurt or abused.

As your child admires and looks up to you so much, do not be surprised if they become upset when you say you will be away from them for an hour, but arrive some hours later, only to hear or discover that your child waited up or stayed by the window for hours, pining for you to return.

It is to your advantage to be aware also that children don't have the same sense of time as adults do. To leave a baby alone in a room for what may be in reality, a matter of minutes, may seem like a lifetime for a baby.

You have to recognise that your baby or young child has no sense of time in the way adults do. To be left alone when they are totally reliant on you, even for just a few moments, can seem to them as though they have been abandoned and that is an incredibly tortuous and terrible thought for a young child to experience.

Only gradually over time, as a result of repetitive experiences of you coming back to your child, do they begin to accept that you will not abandon them, but this takes time to be achieved.

Bear in mind also that if you do not see your child regularly, either because your child is not living with you, or because you are not maintaining regular contact with them, your child won't be able to hold neutral or blank thoughts in connection with your absence in their life.

It will then be very easy for your ex-partner to feed your child negative thoughts about you, if that is what they are inclined to do. It is easy because your child will wonder why you do not see them regularly and even if your ex-partner behaves totally appropriately towards you and does not seek to denigrate you, your child will form ideas about why you are so infrequently in their life.

These ideas are likely to be based around the view that they did something wrong to make you not want to be with them, or that they are simply not loved or lovable.

What I want you to take away from digesting this information is the importance of seeing your child consistently (even when it may be painful or difficult).

If for any reason, you are not able to see them, your child needs a reasonable explanation about why this is the case. They should not be left to try and figure this out for themselves since they will inevitably come up with a reason which is negative or harmful to their self-image.

You would need to provide your child with a clear explanation prior to the expected contact time, so that they were not left waiting in vain for you to arrive. It is likely that you may need to explain to your child on several occasions why you were not able to make contact at a certain date, and reinforce the message that you love them.

The purpose of you reiterating your reasons for missing any contact or time with your child, is to reassure them that they are still very much in your thoughts and that they are still loved. In this way you can help promote a sense of security and self-worth within them.

Obviously, in the event that you are not able to keep a meeting or time spent with your child, you need to inform the other parent, or whoever is caring for your child, and provide them with suitable notice.

Whether you like your ex-partner or the carer of your child is irrelevant, in the sense that no matter what you feel in regard to them, they need to know this information so that they can plan their life and the life of your child adequately.

As a non-resident parent of your child you will need to demonstrate in all the evidence that is brought before the court, that you conduct yourself in a manner that indicates that you are able to put your child's needs first in every respect.

Just so that you are clear, there is no point in demonstrating how able you are to meet your child's emotional needs and then behaving abusively to the other parent who your child lives with.

Remember that you cannot behave in this way without in some way harming your child and in the process harming your family court case.

If you are the resident parent as opposed to the parent the child spends time with, all the matters discussed above about meeting and considering your child's emotional needs, apply equally to you.

You should never attempt to stop, or undermine your child's contact with your ex-partner. The only time it is justifiable to try to prevent your child from seeing the other parent, is when you have strong reasons to believe your ex-partner is, or will likely cause harm to your child and if so, you will need evidence to support your opinions.

If you have taken any notice of what I have documented above concerning the extent to which your child is dependent upon his or her parents and is extremely sensitive to your actions, you will know why it is very detrimental to your child's health and wellbeing to take actions which stop, or jeopardise their time with their other parent.

The same issues apply to you as apply to the non-resident parent.

If for example, there is a good reason why your child can't make the usual contact time, then you need to inform the other parent as soon as possible and explain the reason for this.

You really need to show that you recognise the time spent with the other parent as valuable to your child. It is irrelevant what you feel towards your ex-partner or whether you consider your ex-partner fails to spend any quality time with your child.

Your job is to ensure that your child spends time with the other parent. You do not always know what that time means to your child. Remember that your child knowing you and your attitude towards your ex-partner, may not choose to tell or show you how important it is to them.

What you need to be able to show the court is that you are someone who takes your child's needs seriously and can be consistently relied upon to do so, even if you don't get on well with your ex-partner.

I have spent a fair amount of time discussing your child's emotional needs because your child's emotional needs, wishes and feelings, are perhaps much less instantly visible generally than their physical needs.

You can tell for instance, whether your child needs a bath, their clothes are dirty, or they are hungry or exhausted, by just looking at them. Their emotional feelings and needs generally require you to spend much more time and thought on them, than the cursory glance from which you can glean their physical state.

Earlier, I made the statement that your needs and wants are very different from those of your child's and this is aptly illustrated when comparing your child's emotional needs with your own.

If you argue, or worse still fight with the other parent (or your ex-partner) although it may be upsetting, it is not a massive thing or event to you. You can probably shrug it off in next to no time. For your child however, especially if it is the first argument or altercation he or she has witnessed and they are very young, it will have a massive impact on them. They are likely to be frozen, highly distressed or traumatised by observing such a spectacle.

You have to bear in mind, and be constantly conscious of the fact, that for your child, you and the other parent have an almost god-like status to them.

You are not only much larger and stronger than them, but the fact is that they rely on you for almost everything. In short, you and the other parent, are their world in a very real sense. When you and the other parent are fighting or arguing, your child's stability, security, safety, health and sense of wellbeing are all threatened.

Whilst it may be the cause of some upset to you, for your child it is the equivalent of his or her entire world being at war or in conflict.

Consider also, and burn it into your memory, that your child, because they are a child, does not have the benefit of being able to compare you and your ex-partner with other parents.

You represent their world, so whatever you do – the life you expose them to, becomes the lens with which they view the world.

If you think about that for just a few moments, you will realise just how influential you are in shaping the world that your child sees and comes to accept as normal.

By exposing your child to arguments, conflict or violence, on a habitual basis, the impact will eventually be that your child not only sees conflict and hostility as a normal way of behaviour, but they will view the world as an unsafe place because that is the way they have learned to see the world.

By exposing your child to arguments and conflict you are also inadvertently teaching them to emulate your behaviour when they grow up.

When, following an argument or fight with your ex-partner, you prevent your child from seeing their other parent simply because you are hurt, due to spite or because you are unhappy with them, what you are doing is harming and being spiteful to your child.

Yes, you may be hurting your ex-partner, but you are doing even greater damage to your child, who does not deserve this punishment, but bears the brunt of the pain and is confused about what is going on.

Remember that you and your ex-partner are already adults. You are not emotionally dependent on each other or to your parents in the way that your children are to you and your ex-partner.

You and your ex-partner are their world and they remain acutely conscious of and sensitive to how you as parents treat each other and behave towards others.

I have explained how your child is emotionally impacted by actions you can take without necessarily being aware of how sensitive your child is to your behaviour or actions.

The second quote at the beginning of this chapter by Virginia Satir, I consider, eloquently illustrates just how vulnerable and sensitive children are, not just to what you say, or how you behave, but also to your facial expressions or body language.

Your children pick up and very accurately interpret, your facial expressions, your mood, thoughts and feelings. Children are often described as sponges, in that they regularly absorb or soak up everything you show them or expose them to.

It is for this reason that you need to be highly conscious of and vigilant regarding how you speak or behave with regard to the other parent or any other person.

Your child being highly sensitive to your feelings and thoughts, will also pick up how you feel about them. Every subtle hint or fine distinction in your body language, expressions or gesture, is observed and correctly interpreted by your child.

You need to become very conscious of how easily your real thoughts and attitudes are transferred to your child and the impact of this transference of your feelings on their sense of wellbeing. Frequently, as the quote above suggests, parents are not aware of the many messages that they are sending out, that are being clearly received by their children continually.

If you are not aware of the messages you are sending, you are not well placed to recognise the impact your messages have on your child's self-image.

Basically then, to be able to meet your child's emotional needs, the court would want you to demonstrate, by the way you behave and the decisions you make, that you are able to see things from your child's point of view and are able to act in accordance with what their needs are.

Children need to know and feel that they are wanted, loved, appreciated and valued.

Your child also needs to have a definite sense of who is part of their family.

I have argued that it is less helpful to see your child as a possession, but instead as someone you have duties and responsibilities toward.

Your child will want and need to develop a sense of belonging to those in their family and this is very important for them.

One of the very worst things you can do to your child is denying them the knowledge of who their birth mother or birth father is.

It is nothing short of devastating for any child to discover that the person who they thought was their mother or father in fact was not.

The longer or older a child is when they receive this earth-shattering news, the more devastating and harmful it is for them. Children do not need to feel confused about who their birth parents are or were. They need clear knowledge in this regard.

Can you imagine what it would feel like to hear that the person you thought was your mother or father, was not your real birth parent?

If, as I have argued, you are your child's world, then to discover that you are not their birth parent may be comparable to their world imploding. To hear such news, would threaten the very core of their security, stability and sense of identity.

To withhold such information from your child would be a highly selfish and destructive act. To fail to provide your child with this information is not an act of compassion and it is certainly not in your child's best interests. It cannot be, because in so doing you are not sparing them from harm. You are ensuring that they will experience harm later, whenever they discover the truth.

In the same way that children need to know who their birth parents are, under normal and most circumstances, they also need to know and have contact with their siblings, whether they are full siblings or not.

It pays to always remember that your child is a product of two parents and thus unless there are very good reasons, your child should know, and spend time with their siblings and other family members, from both sides of their family.

As well as their physical and emotional needs, your child needs to have his or her educational needs met.

As you know, it is expected that your child should attend school punctually and regularly. If they are to get the most out of their educational experiences and opportunities.

Let me reiterate, that I am not just talking about what you will need to demonstrate when you are in the witness box, but I am referring to how you will need to present, in every respect throughout your court case, and then throughout your life.

Key Learning Points

- Your child's needs are separate from yours. You have to have the capacity to distinguish between the two.
- Good parents have the ability to see things from their child's viewpoint and demonstrate empathy and flexibility.
- Children have a strong need to have a sense of belonging. Imagine the devastation caused to a child who discovers that the person they have become used to seeing as their parent, is

not their birth parent. It is vital they are given honest information as soon as possible.

- Good parenting entails prioritising your child's needs above those of your own.
- It is not enough to meet your child's physical needs, it is absolutely vital that you meet your child's emotional needs for attention, affection, praise, stimulation, encouragement, security, safety and consistency.
- Be aware of the messages you are regularly sending out to your child. Make sure those messages are ones that pick your child up and fill them with the certainty that they are loved and lovable, rather than ones that put them down and keep them there throughout their life.
- Children want to feel valued and worthy of your love. If you criticise them often and fail to offer warmth and spend quality time with them, they will likely grow up feeling unloved and unworthy of being loved.
- Supply your child with clear information about their life and explain any absence/s from their life in a way that lets them know they are loved, and that it was not their fault. Do not just blame the other parent.

- You occupy an extremely influential position with regard to your child. Be mindful of this and act accordingly with your child's wants and feelings at the forefront of your mind and behaviour.
- Never abuse the other parent or malign their character. In doing so, you cause substantial damage to your child.
- Children have a variety of needs but what they need most from you is your understanding, encouragement, love, time and flexibility, especially, as they grow and develop.
- Your capacity to understand your child's needs will be dependent on your own experiences of being parented.
- In order for children to get the best out of the educational system, they need to attend school punctually and regularly and they will need you to offer them routines and clear boundaries in the process.

Responsibility

We cannot solve a problem by saying 'It's not my problem.' We cannot solve a problem by hoping that someone else will solve it for us. I can solve a problem only when I say 'This is my problem and it is up to me to solve it.' But many, so many, seek to avoid the pain of their problems by saying to themselves: 'This problem was caused by other people, or by social circumstances beyond my control and therefore it is up to other people or society to solve this problem for me. It is not really my personal problem.'

M. Scott Peck The Road Less Travelled.

"Once you have accepted your flaws, no one can use them against you."

Tyrion Lannister Game of Thrones.

How many times have you heard someone say, "It's not my problem?"

You hear children, teenagers, parents, partners, relatives, friends, colleagues, supervisors, managers, bosses, politicians and leaders all over the world saying those same words on a regular basis.

Is it any wonder then, that you learn to pass on, or try to pass on your responsibility to someone else?

When doing so, what frequently accompanies this, is your desire to pass the responsibility for any problem on to another person, and a willingness to blame them.

This also, perhaps, comes as no surprise since you can often hear in the media people being asked "who is to blame for this problem."

It's as if by identifying someone to blame, that the problem will disappear.

But of course the reality is much different. You can't just point the finger at someone and then forget about the problem.

In my view, it is such a short-sighted, fundamentally selfish and flawed approach to any problem, because it seeks to deny responsibility.

When you don't take responsibility for something, and seek to blame others, your ability to find a suitable solution to the problem is rendered pretty much impossible because the attitude adopted precludes you from looking at the problem from all angles.

Sadly, seeking to find those culpable, is the way politicians and leaders behave and this filters down to you and I. But doing so never results in long term, positive results because it exacerbates the problem, causing resentment and distrust with others.

It cannot lead to finding a satisfactory solution, because in so doing you have removed an important component, or at least part of the problem. You cannot solve a problem that you are part of by taking yourself out of the equation and blaming someone else.

Unfortunately, that is the way people seem to want to behave. It's as if they think, by doing so the problem has vanished. Of course, it is only a matter of time before it rears its head again, and the blamed person, or party has now learned, or chosen to point their finger straight at you.

Then what follows is a pretty pointless argument of tit for tat, with both parties blaming the other, while the situation remains unresolved. In the meantime, it is your children who pay the price for their parents' short-sighted behaviour.

Unfortunately, it often feels so much easier to deny and deflect, rather than accept responsibility or at least your part of the responsibility for a particular problem.

I think that from an early age we have learned to avoid taking responsibility for issues which affect us or others, and by doing so, we teach our children the same defective response.

If you're going to give yourself a real chance of improving anything that affects you and that you play a part in, you have to begin by looking at yourself.

There is a famous Michael Jackson record (Man In The Mirror) which captures this point so eloquently. So start by looking at the man in the mirror!

We are human beings and thus all capable of error, but that's no reason to compound it, by making the same mistakes over and over again. After you have argued, or disagreed vehemently with someone, make the effort to reflect and see where you may have been at fault. Start by looking at yourself first.

I am not saying that you, or anyone else is wrong or blameworthy with regard to your argument, I am suggesting that there are better ways of managing problems and I am stating that blaming people is rarely, if ever helpful.

Although I am suggesting that you look at yourself or your actions, I am not suggesting you blame yourself either. If anything, I am advising you to remove the desire or tendency to seek to blame others or yourself from your behaviour.

Seek instead to understand yourself and to understand the actions of others, by attempting to put yourself in their place. That is the best way to understand others and in doing so, we learn to understand ourselves better.

Our failure to accept responsibility and to go on to blame others, results in the problem persisting for far longer and being far more destructive than it needed to be.

One of the places this can so often be observed is the relationship between former partners, parents, or in the relationship, between parent/s and social workers.

When you fail to recognise your own responsibility for events or incidents, you have the potential to cause a lot of harm to your child and your court case because you may be resistant to looking properly at the problem and the consequences associated with it.

It is difficult to take responsibility for the problems you face, but the long term consequences of refusing to acknowledge your responsibility for making decisions or, bringing about the circumstances faced by you and your child, can never be fully palmed off onto someone else.

Even if you were in an abusive relationship and your former partner readily acknowledged that they were abusive to you. You still have to ask yourself questions about why you chose the person you did?

Why you chose to have a child with them?

Why you remained in the relationship for the length of time you did?

What part you played in bringing about the current situation?

How or in which ways did you act to safeguard your child?

In which ways have you given your ex-partner the impression that this abuse would be tolerated?

How much conflict and abuse has your child really observed or been exposed to?

Have you been in denial concerning the abuse?

Have you sought professional or any type of help regarding it?

What is there about you that has attracted this sort of behaviour from a partner?

What other, if any, abusive relationships have you chosen to be in?

In what ways did your childhood predispose you to accepting an abusive relationship?

What will be the long term and cumulative impact on your child from being exposed to this type of abusive behaviour?

The above are just a selection of questions I have thrown together which I hope provide you with some insight concerning your responsibility in giving rise to these circumstances.

I have chosen the scenario of you being a victim of domestic abuse and the very unlikely full acceptance of this by your ex-partner, because I wanted to highlight that even under those circumstances, you still would have to accept some responsibility for what has gone on.

Although it is natural to rush to absolve ourselves from responsibility and censure, since no one likes to feel blamed or burdened by responsibility, we never really grow up and take charge of our problems, without accepting our culpability and taking steps to put things right.

Whether you take this seriously or not, you can be sure that your ex-partner's lawyer, or the local authority lawyer will. They will have done their homework and you will almost definitely be posed questions designed to expose your failure, to accept responsibility for whatever the current circumstances are.

Parents who fail to accept responsibility for their actions, invariably present negatively at court, and this does not bode well for the future.

If by the time you attend court, you have not yet figured out, or are not yet fully cognizant of your role, as regards the circumstances, in which your child is having to cope with, then you have given the court no reason to believe that you are willing and able to change things for the better currently or in the future.

Since, if you fail to realise there is a problem, you will have little or no motivation to tackle a problem you have no awareness of.

As the quote by Tyrion Lannister says: "*if you have accepted your flaws, they cannot be used against you.*"

This assumes of course, that you have devoted the time to identify your shortcomings, you have acknowledged them, and armed with the knowledge of your flaws, made the necessary adjustments and changes to your character and behaviour, to adequately address them.

All of this is much more easily said than done. It would require you to have the necessary insight, the motivation and willingness to change, the support of others, professional or otherwise, and the time to do it.

Put simply, accepting your responsibility, in my view, equates with having an appropriate attitude, towards your child and your court case.

Having a good attitude is extremely important when preparing for and attending court. Your attitude determines your thoughts, feelings, actions and ultimately your results.

If for example you intend to pass a test, present well at an interview, or perform well at any task, your state of mind or attitude, and the responsibility you assume for undertaking the task, is key to your success.

The more responsibility you accept for your entire situation, the greater the chance of you being able to sort it out properly. The less responsibility you accept, the less likely you are to fully resolve the issue.

Your attitude then, or willingness to assume full responsibility, will determine your behaviour and likely your result.

What I also want you to consider, in fact, I suggest you etch it into your thoughts, is that when you are going through the court process, and especially when you give your evidence, your behaviour is under the scrutiny of the court and your attitude is immediately obvious.

If you have a bad or negative attitude, it is instantly recognisable. Just as, if you have a good or positive attitude, that too cannot fail to be observed by the audience of the court.

Since the difference between a good attitude and a bad one is as clearly demarcated and immediately as obvious as day and night.

So it is your responsibility to choose to have a good attitude and do all in your power to rid yourself of any behaviour, thoughts or actions associated with a bad attitude.

How can you tell if you have a good or a bad attitude?

Well...your attitude is not something you developed yesterday. Instead it is something you have developed over many years – it is habitual and so much a part of you, that it may be very difficult for you to identify it.

But if you take your time and think about how you respond to others and how they respond to you, you may be able to begin to pick up ideas about the type of attitude you have.

Attitudes are recognisable without even saying a word, they relate to the thoughts you hold in your head, which are observable via the behaviour, actions or inaction that you take

Another way of discovering the type of attitude you have is by reflecting on past events, incidents or disagreements with others and questioning how much responsibility you took for past differences of opinion or arguments with others.

This is not at all easy to do and I think you will find it very helpful to seek out and request the help of someone who is willing and able to be honest with you.

Seek out and identify someone you know, who knows you well and, has no fear of telling you the truth. Obviously this person should not be someone who has a vested interest in telling you whatever you might want to hear.

Having found this person, you may not like what they have to say, but it will be invaluable to you, in the event that you make the time, and commitment to learn from whatever feedback they offer you.

So often it is the people who need this help most who choose to ignore it at their own peril and of course, the peril of their children.

A good way to discover vital information about your attitude is to consider how you respond to complaints or criticisms. How you respond to criticism (even more so than complaints) can speak volumes, about your attitude.

No one likes to be criticised or receive complaints but it's how you react or respond to such responses which says so much about you and your attitude.

When dealing with others, it is always beneficial to adopt the practice of trying to see things from the other person's perspective. Look at things from their viewpoint and then ask yourself honestly, what you would do, or how you would see things, if you were them.

What I am asking you to do requires that you take the time, make the effort and employ the skill of empathy. But it is well worth your time and effort, because if you make a habit of doing so, it will save you a great deal of frustration, pain, time, money, relationship problems, and health concerns in the future.

If you begin to realise that your attitude needs much improvement, then no one but you can do anything about it. You have to become aware of this. It's your responsibility to decide to improve your attitude, being conscious of the reality that you can stand out in people's minds due to the degree of inadequacy of your attitude, or amaze them with the sheer brilliance of your positive mental state.

The choice and responsibility is all yours.

But if you decide that you need to improve your attitude, as well as enlist the help of a friend who will be honest with you, you need to be prepared to listen and to develop the self-discipline to make the required changes.

Self-discipline and self-control will definitely be required by you in abundance in the event that you seek to positively influence your attitude and, to improve your attitude, you will need to master and control your emotions.

Key Learning Points

- You can never solve a problem by denying or ignoring your responsibility in creating it.
- You can never solve a problem or make things better by blaming someone else or seeking to do so.

- You can start by looking at yourself and accepting that you are not perfect and that as humans we all make mistakes
- Attempt to put yourself in the other person's shoes and see things from their point of view.
- When you walk in another person's shoes, you not only understand them better, but you understand yourself better.
- When you fail to accept responsibility for a situation you had a part in creating, you advertise or announce your poor attitude.
- Poor attitudes or states of mind result in poor results or outcomes and are immediately obvious to those observing you.
- If you want to maximise your chance of obtaining a good outcome, choose to have a good attitude. The court can't help but notice it.
- Good attitudes need to be developed, they do not materialise overnight. You may need the help of an honest friend to identify your overall state of mind.
- No one other than you is responsible for the attitude you hold.

Controlling Your Emotions

"To balance and take control of our emotions, is one of the most important tasks in life."

Dr T.P. Chia

"Calmness of mind is one of the beautiful jewels of wisdom. It is the result of long and patient effort in self-control."

James Allen

I am going to begin this chapter, by telling you something that is very simple to say, and very true, but at the same time, not at all easy to do.

Quite simply, if you do not learn to control your emotions, then your emotions will control you and when you are in the court environment, and particularly when you are giving evidence, if you can't control your emotions, you will easily be controlled by whoever is cross-examining you.

Controlling your emotions and maintaining a positive attitude or state of mind is of fundamental importance, particularly when being cross-examined, because if your emotions are triggered, you will not be able to think clearly or give a reasoned response, and it will be visible to all concerned that you are not in control of your feelings.

However, managing to master your feelings, is so much harder to do than say, for many reasons. Often it is due to the habitual behaviour we have learnt from childhood experiences and because we rarely take the time and effort to make the required changes to our attitude in later life.

You may not appreciate, what I am going to tell you, but I'm going to say it anyway, not because I get enjoyment from saying things that you might find annoying or upsetting, but instead because I believe if you're going to get the best out of this book, you are going to have to confront, and deal with behaviours that have almost certainly become habitual.

You're going to have to face the fact that there are many things that happen to you during your lifetime and some, if not many, of these things are painful things, that can scar you emotionally and psychologically.

Some of these experiences and incidents will have been traumatic and highly damaging to you at a time in your life when you were very vulnerable, dependent and too young to do anything about it.

I am referring to events in your life, such as living with a parent who self-harms; or parents who abuse alcohol or drugs; parents who abuse or neglect you; parents or carers who expose you to their domestic abuse; parents who are sadly suffering with mental ill health, and reject or abandon you.

Events such as these and others in your early life can leave you hurt, damaged, traumatised, angry, resentful, insecure, petrified, feeling unloved and unworthy of love. They may have affected how you see yourself, your life, and what you give to life and expect from it.

These experiences and events may have happened many years ago, but what you may not realise is just how much events such as these, as well as other, later painful experiences, have shaped, and may be continuing to shape your life.

Unless you are really very different from the average person, these painful experiences, although having occurred a long time ago, are events that when you think back to them, still easily, if not instantly, bring back vivid memories, as if they had happened just yesterday.

If you doubt what I am saying, take your time to think back to a painful experience that happened long ago, and you may be surprised how quickly all the old feelings, emotions, images, scents, sounds or tastes come flooding back to you.

Why might this be the case, you may ask?

Well there are at least two reasons I can think of:

Firstly, it is the case, because you (and when I say you I mean that we) all tend to think more easily about negative things and things that hurt us, rather than positive things. We tend to keep those memories alive by thinking about them and thereby reinforcing the memory of it, and a well-rehearsed rationale, for justifying why we are what we are.

Secondly, it is because you tend to do nothing to address the event or incidents that had such a powerful impact on you. Maybe this is the case because you don't know what to do. Or, as is perhaps more likely the case, you don't recognise the need to do anything, to address the painful or traumatic experiences from your past.

It no doubt seems easier for you (and here, you are not at all alone, since the vast majority of people seem to think in the same way) to come to the conclusion, that whatever occurred in your earlier life is past and has no lasting or continued impact on you today.

You will no doubt have heard some people say in hindsight with regard to a traumatic event, such as your parents separating, or you being physically beaten, that it didn't do them any harm.

But the problem with that argument is that because those events happened to you so long ago, they have become a normal experience for you. You have grown up having, lived through that experience, and so naturally that experience has coloured, or impacted who you are today.

The point I am making to you is, you are not always best placed to reach the decision that you were not harmed by what happened to you years ago, because you don't know who you would have been and/or how you would have felt about such events if they had not become, an integral part of your life.

If what I am saying makes no sense to you because you can't understand how it is possible that you are considered not best placed to come to the conclusion that you weren't harmed by those events, then let me try to explain it this way.

You, I and everyone else, are who we are today, or view things in the way we do, because of the dominant, daily influences that we were exposed to in our childhood.

These influences were not 'one off,' or occasional occurrences. They were instead habitual influences that occurred over and over again, so frequently, that they became 'normal' behaviour.

That is the reason why, if you were raised in a household where you were routinely physically beaten, you may well have learned to hold the opinion that it is an acceptable way, to discipline children.

If you grew up in another household, and let's say, that this parent or carer did not beat you, then the dominating influences that you see and experience daily would be such that they influence you to think and feel in an entirely different way than you likely would do, if you had grown up regularly being beaten.

In other words, what you consider to be normal behaviour (with this different parent or carer) would be very different from what you would likely consider to be normal behaviour, if growing up in a household where being beaten is a normal practice.

What I am inviting you to consider is that you can become used to anything if you are exposed to it often and long enough.

Children are initially terrified when they first see parents arguing and fighting. If you have ever observed young children, witnessing their parents or adults engaged in violent behaviour, you will probably have noticed that they freeze because they are petrified.

But if children see it often enough, they begin to become de-sensitised to it and if they continue to be exposed to it, eventually it becomes accepted by them, as 'normal,' everyday behaviour.

Whatever you see as 'normal' behaviour, is that which has become habitual, such that you tend not to question it, since it is behaviour you are very used to and has become so much a part of your life, that you may be inclined to dismiss discussions about new or different behaviour as pointless.

I suggest that you may then not be in a position to objectively evaluate it because the lens with which you view things, may be unable to detect where, your vision has become (due to habitual exposure) skewed.

It is really important that you grasp this information and are able to become reflective concerning your own childhood experiences, because parents who are unable to do this, often appear to have difficulty putting themselves in their child's position. They lack the understanding and insight to show empathy.

It's essential because empathy is a key skill in parenting and if you fail to show this understanding and empathy with regard to your own parenting experiences, you are unlikely to demonstrate this empathy towards your children and this will be observed by the judge, and those who will be engaged, in cross-examining you.

I cannot emphasise this point, to you strongly enough.

Being engaged in family court proceedings (private or public law) without having taken the time and effort to examine and evaluate the way you were parented, and the way you parent your own child, is akin to attending a job interview that is vital to your ambitions, without having thoroughly prepared for the questions likely to be posed to you.

It is very easy for you to come to the conclusion that you don't need to address any distressing events that happened in your earlier life and this I believe, is because you and I live or exist in a culture where there remains a stigma against receiving therapy from a counsellor or an appropriate therapist.

You have probably learnt to see going to a therapist or counsellor as a sign of weakness - that you are unwell, or at least, as an acknowledgement that you are in the need of help.

But isn't it the truth that we are all in need of help in one way or another?

Choose any area of life that you want to focus on and I am sure you will recognise that we are all, whilst competent in some areas, in need of much help in other areas.

Now am I really saying that you need to see a counsellor or therapist?

I have no way of knowing, because I don't know you.

But what I can advise you is, if you consider what I have documented in the last chapter on parenting to be nonsense, if you recognise no value in what I have written in this chapter, then I think there is a very high chance that you need to think very carefully about your parenting experiences and parenting style or values.

I am not telling you this because I have documented what is written above and therefore it must be right, because I said so. I have instead, merely tried to provide you with information about parenting that I hope and expect to be useful to you in preparing for and presenting your evidence at court, since it is this parenting knowledge and principles which I have successfully relied upon to guide me through innumerable family court cases.

If you do reach the conclusion that perhaps your parenting experiences whilst you were a child were, or, are not helpful to you currently, there are alternatives to counselling or professional therapeutic help.

Today there are lots of self-help books, parenting courses, coaching, seminars, information and advice you can access online and offline that can offer you the help you need or at least point you in the direction you may need to go.

The point I am making to you is that if up until this point you believed you had a good reason for failing to manage your emotions well and allowing your feelings to dictate your behaviour, you now have a very good reason to do something different.

Although gaining full control of your emotions is likely to take some time to achieve, you can begin right away to start mastering your emotions.

There is nothing like having a good reason, or motivation to make necessary changes to your life, and there are few stronger motivations, than taking action to support and protect, your child or children.

So, how can you start?

What do you need to do differently?

One of the first things you can do (whether you know you are someone who, shall we say, does not always show the best attitude, or not) is to practice, getting into a positive, or good state.

When you are in a good state of mind, you have more of a 'can do' attitude. You have a much more energetic demeanour or manner that provides you with the drive to do, whatever you need to do.

Contrast this with a mental attitude which complains that you 'can't be bothered' to do what you need to do, or with a manner that whines, saying something to the effect of, "that's long."

What you are really saying is, you can't be bothered to put in the time and energy necessary, to adopt the type of attitude required, to present as well as you can.

Essentially, although you may not want to recognise it, you are unwilling to do what's necessary for your child.

Let's face it, if you have to go to court to give evidence concerning your child, you might as well not bother to attend court if you can't muster the energy to prepare properly for it, because getting into a good mental state and remaining in a good state is critical to how you come across in the witness box.

So, how do you raise or improve your mental state of mind or attitude?

There are probably lots of ways you can achieve this, below are just some ways which sprung to mind.

You can play your favourite piece of music – something that is uplifting or inspirational.

Close your eyes, take several deep breaths, and picture yourself on a beach, on a sunny day under a palm tree, watching the waves roll in and roll out again.

Or with closed eyes, see yourself at a place of peace and tranquillity.

You could read an inspirational poem, or read inspirational quotes.

You could watch an influential video or film, read inspirational articles, or self-help books, designed to get you to tune in to, and harness the hidden power within you.

You could watch someone you admire greatly. Maybe a great sportsman or athlete that you hold in high regard that puts you in a great space whenever you watch them perform.

You could also think about or reminisce about a time or experience in your life when you had a great victory, or succeeded at something important to you. Each great experience you achieved, or success you gained, is a reminder of what you can achieve, whenever you decide to put your heart and mind into a worthwhile pursuit.

Think back to how you felt, when you were offered a job you wanted, received applause for something you did, were offered praise or recognition, for your efforts and results.

Or perhaps, when you stood up to someone who was a bit of a bully, or you protected someone else who was being threatened or taken advantage of.

Think about how you feel after doing exercise, or visualising yourself in a place of awesome, natural beauty.

Basically, do what you need to do to create that state of mind you need.

All of these uplifting times, experiences and events, are things you can use to improve your state of mind and if you identify things that work well for you, you need to use them regularly.

As you can perhaps imagine, it is not difficult to find things that help uplift us. What is much more challenging, yet crucial, to your presentation at court, is your ability to **remain** in a positive state of mind, throughout your time in the witness box.

You have to maintain your composure at all times, despite any provocative posturing, or questions from the lawyer, or lawyers cross-examining you.

Bear in mind also that the judge can ask you questions whenever he or she wants to. Normally they do so to clarify, or get clear in their mind, what you are saying. But there may well be occasions when the judge decides to ask or say things that may irritate you.

What I want you to understand, and engrave into your thoughts is this: whilst you are in the witness box, you can be asked anything and you may not like the way it is asked, or what is being inferred, by whoever is asking you the question.

You may feel insulted, angered, abused and disrespected.

None of that is important. Do you really think that displaying your anger and annoyance at the lawyer, or the judge, is going to help you to be seen as someone giving credible evidence?

What is important for you is how you handle or cope with whatever is thrown at you.

To put it another way, what I want you to consider, is that it is not what happens to you in life that is important. **What is much more important is, how you respond to what happens to you.**

You cannot control the things that occur outside of you, the things that are beyond your control. What you can, and must control is how you respond inside to whatever happens to you.

To lose your temper or react with anger or frustration, will not benefit you in any way.

Firstly, it will provide the judge with an unfavourable opinion of you. They will likely form the impression that you are easily irritated and that will not bode well for you.

Secondly, it will send a very clear signal to the lawyer cross-examining you, that you are about to explode and their tactics are working well. As a result, you are very likely to receive more of the same type of posturing and questions which infuriated you in the first place.

Thirdly, if you react with anger, you are much less likely to be able to think clearly and answer the questions in a thought out, or reasonable manner.

Fourthly, by reacting in this way, it will undermine your previous or earlier written evidence, as the last thing you would want to demonstrate in your written evidence (statement/s) is that you are someone who easily becomes irate.

Finally, if you are unable to control your emotions, you will likely experience considerable difficulty with being able to listen to the question and subsequent questions, because it is very difficult to re-compose yourself and get back into the state of mind you need to be in throughout being cross-examined.

You have to develop the capacity to maintain your composure following answering each question, so that you can answer each new question in a thoughtful or considered manner.

The lawyer cross-examining you, knows that for most people, they only have to trip you up on one occasion, to result in you losing your composure, or self-control.

They know that it takes an effort of will and concentration to continue to remain serene throughout being cross-examined and so the easiest way to disturb your concentration is to 'rattle' you, by posing questions, or behaving in a manner, designed to put you, on the defensive. Your job, or at least a big part of your job, is to ensure you show no outward sign of losing control and the best way to ensure this, is to inwardly remain in control of yourself.

Once you react in a defensive manner, you are already on a fast and slippery slope to destruction, since it is very difficult to recover your self-control in the witness box, once you have lost it.

Mastering your emotions is something, you must learn to do at all costs if you want to be seen as someone giving credible, if not, cogent evidence.

The responsibility for mastering your emotions and maintaining a positive attitude and state of mind, rests with no one else but you. There is no one else who can do it, or who can ensure it will happen, except you.

But what if, as far as you are concerned, your attitude is fine? What if you consider, that it's other people's attitudes that need to change and not yours?

In that case, you are unlikely to be motivated to improve your attitude and in the event that your self-perception differs markedly from how others perceive you, this will likely spell disaster for you at the family court.

So, how do you gain insight into how others perceive you when your view may differ markedly from theirs?

How do you develop the motivation to change or improve yourself, when currently you see no impetus to do so?

I think a model that may be of assistance to you is called the Johari Window, which I shall briefly elucidate in a few moments.

But prior to doing so, and by way of introducing you to this model, I am going to ask you to do something that I imagine most, if not all of us, do every day.

I am going to ask you to look at yourself in a mirror for a few moments. Then I am going to ask you to consider what thoughts come to mind from what you see? The reason I have asked you to do this, is because no matter what you look like, most of us, I believe, will see things about our physical appearance that we would like to alter or improve.

When you look in a mirror you see, or you take notice of your physical appearance. In other words, how you think you appear to others. Your attention is riveted on how you look on the outside.

But your physical attributes make up only a part of how you present to others and I would argue that a much larger, or more significant part of how you present to others, relates to character, as opposed to looks.

Have you ever, for instance, observed someone you consider to be 'drop dead gorgeous?' They are the most beautiful man or woman you could ever imagine and for a time you are in ecstasy at the mere idea of thinking about them.

But then, the bubble bursts. They open their mouth and their words are vile and vulgar. Or their behaviour simply does not match up to the fantasy you constructed about them.

If this resonates with an experience of yours, then you will know exactly what I mean. Physical appearance is the first thing we see that may attract us but after that, other factors become more important.

If it's true that other factors become more important, then wouldn't you agree that it is unwise to devote your time to merely to addressing your physical appearance alone?

So, why do we tend to do so?

Perhaps we are inclined to do so because we are used to focusing on our exterior presentation, we are self-conscious about what is immediately visible to us and unaware of other important factors.

We see the physical aspects of our appearance that we want to make better, but cannot see, or fail to focus attention on, aspects of our personality or character we need to improve.

But what you fail to see or are unable to pay attention to, is not only observable to others but is also palpable to them.

Think about that for a moment!

That means that others can, not only see things about you that you do not see, but they also feel and experience things in connection with you or your behaviour that you have no awareness of.

Now of course this is not just true as regards you, it is true of all of us to some degree. You can, I am sure, identify aspects to other people's character that they have no awareness of or insight into. So if it is true with regard to other people, it is equally true in connection with you.

In my view then, this is a mistake that we can all make but we do so at our peril, especially as it relates to family law court cases, because those scrutinising you cannot help but see who you are and how you impact on others.

It is who you really are, or at least the perception of who you are, that those scrutinising you will see and not how you think you appear to others.

To aid you in seeing yourself as others see you, as mentioned earlier, the Johari Window model is a useful tool you can use to enhance your self-awareness, your relationship with yourself and others. The Johari Window was developed by psychologists Joseph Luft and Harrington Ingham in 1955.

You will see below that there are four areas, or quadrants which represent combinations of knowledge and/or lack of knowledge about you.

The first area (in the top left hand corner) is known as Open space, in that it is knowledge about you or your behaviour which is both known to you and to others. You can think of this quadrant as representing public knowledge about you.

For example, that you are a black male, six feet tall.

The second area (top right hand corner) can be referred to as the Blindspot and it represents an area where you are not aware of certain matters or behaviour, whilst others are.

An example of this could be that you have bad breath or that in your interpersonal relationships you never accept that you make errors.

The third area (bottom left hand corner) is the Hidden area. This represents an area of knowledge that is hidden or unknown to others but is known to you. It is perhaps, an area you choose to keep to yourself and do not share information about with others.

An example of this might be that you know other languages or that in your spare time you attend acting classes.

In the event that you choose to share this information with another person who you have grown closer to, then the Hidden area moves towards becoming an Open space and it is information that is known and can now be communicated about.

The fourth area is known as the Unknown area because it represents information or knowledge that you do not know about yourself and that others do not know about either.

	Known to self	Known to others
Known to others	Open Area or arena	Blindspot (unknown to you)
Not known to others	Hidden area or façade	Unknown

The Johari Window, Joseph Luft and Harrington Ingham, 1955

As a result there is no communication about this, since no one knows about it.

An example of this could be you becoming an artist or a public speaker when the skills or talents involved were something you would never consider yourself capable of or ever contemplated doing.

As intimated above, these quadrants are not set in stone but can shrink or grow depending on your choice of action. Your Blind spot can decrease if you allow yourself to listen to and act upon feedback or communication that others give you.

Discovering information that others know about you can be invaluable to you. But it needs to be conveyed to you in a sensitive manner, at an appropriate time, preferably in a suitable place and where it can be given confidentially, so that you are willing and able to receive it. In addition, you have to be open enough and prepared to listen to it, reflect on it and benefit from it.

By being able to take on board the feedback given to you by others, your Open area becomes wider and your Blind spot shrinks, as your self-awareness grows.

Your ability to develop trusting relationships with others will be very important here, and the more trust you develop, the more willing you may be to disclose or share hidden information about you, which reduces the Hidden area and again increases the Open area. At the same time, it encourages or gives rise to a safer, more trusting environment.

By communicating more openly and asking for and valuing feedback received, this may lead to you discovering things about yourself that were previously unknown to you and others.

This has the effect of reducing the Unknown quadrant as your level of self-awareness grows.

I hope I have described this model in a way that makes sense to you and that you can use it to develop greater insight into how you behave, who you are, or are perceived to be.

To further assist those of you who require help to see yourself as others see you I have constructed in the next chapter, a number of questions which if you are willing and able to answer them honestly, will provide you with a clearer picture of the attitude you show to the world.

It will probably be of great benefit to you to ask someone who knows you well and who has no vested interest in flattering you, to answer these questions about you.

The answers you receive may not massage your ego, but they will prove invaluable to you, if you wish to see yourself as other people see you, and may also provide you with a strong reason to improve your attitude if necessary.

Key Learning Points

- If you do not learn to control your emotions, your emotions will control you.
- Your dominant attitudes and emotions were likely formed long ago during your childhood via repeated experiences which remain highly relevant to you to this day.

- Rarely, if ever, do we take the time and effort to address painful experiences and trauma that occurred when we were young and vulnerable.
- The impact of these experiences remain with us as adults, influencing our beliefs, norms, values, feelings and attitudes.
- If subjected to continual repeated events, whatever you are exposed to will eventually influence you and become accepted by you as 'normal behaviour.'
- In the event you decide you need to master your emotions, there are many things you can begin to do now, to take charge of your state of mind.
- Choose things you love to do which are habit forming – the challenge is to learn to remain in a positive state of mind.
- The only thing you can control in life, is how you think and feel. What happens in your life is not as important as how you choose to respond to it.
- When you lack composure, get angry, or react defensively, you expose your weaknesses and attract more questions, which likely evoke the same type of responses within you

- There are things that others know about us that we do not know about ourselves.
- We can learn about these things and about ourselves by asking for feedback from others who see things we do not.
- Giving feedback is not always easy to do, it needs to be given with a degree of sensitivity, at appropriate times and in a suitable, confidential venue.
- The more you are able to develop trusting relationships, the more you are likely to learn valuable information about yourself and others.
- Being able to be open and communicative with others ultimately opens your world up to be a safer place.

Self-Analysis Questions

"If your emotional abilities aren't in hand, if you don't have self-awareness, if you are not able to manage your distressing moments, if you can't have empathy and have effective relationships, then no matter how smart you are, you are not going to get very far."

Daniel Goleman.

"*Wisest is she who knows she does not know.*"

Jostein Gaarder, Sophie's World: A Novel About The History Of Philosophy."

In order to protect yourself and simultaneously present well at court, you have to know yourself well. You have to be self-aware – this means being aware of not just your moods or emotion, but also being aware of your thoughts about your mood or emotion. This ability to monitor your feelings and thoughts is an important initial step in developing self-control.

You cannot allow yourself to be swamped by your emotions.

Unfortunately, as Daniel Goleman mentions in his book Emotional Intelligence, those people who are engulfed by their emotions, often feel helpless to get out of thinking about their painful emotions – they are trapped and seem unable to escape from these painful thoughts. This inability to control your emotions and self-soothe yourself has for some people become a habit, or way of life.

If you are to get the best out of this book, you may need to change your thoughts and emotional state of mind whenever you recognise you are thinking and feeling and consumed by negative thoughts and moods. If you do so often enough, it will become a priceless habit that will benefit you when giving evidence and also in innumerable other ways.

The key, however, lies in realising where you are in terms of your dominant emotional state right now.

I hope the questions below assist you in gaining a fairly clear picture of where you are currently at.

Do you often feel that life is not fair?

Do you feel as though the odds are stacked against you?

Would you describe yourself as generally a happy or sad person?

Do you smile often, or hardly ever?

Are you a patient person?

Would your friends say you are understanding?

Are you inclined to give others the benefit of the doubt?

Are you someone who tends to jump to conclusions?

Do you try to get all the information before you act or make up your mind?

Do you often act without thinking first?

Do you find it hard to accept when you are wrong?

When you are wrong, do you apologise?

How difficult is it to say you are sorry?

Do you see apologising as a form of weakness?

How important is it for you to feel you are right?

Do you get angry easily?

Do you calm down swiftly after an argument or smoulder for lengthy periods of time?

Are you told that you often look angry?

Would people say you are easy to talk to?

Are you a good listener?

Do you talk more than you're inclined to listen?

Do you love the sound of your own voice?

Have you ever been told that you think you know it all?

How do you respond when complaints are made about you?

Are you only really interested in what you want?

How often have you been described as selfish?

Do you generally see the wider picture?

Can you see things from other people's point of view?

Do you blame others easily?

Are you inclined to criticise others easily?

How do you respond to criticism?

Can you accept your responsibility when things go wrong?

Do you think honesty is overrated?

Do you tell the occasional lie, or has being untruthful become a way of life?

How fairly do you treat others?

Can you justify treating others unfairly?

Do you routinely treat others unfairly?

How do you treat people who are subordinate to you?

Do you make excuses instead of being honest with yourself?

How often do you lack the energy to do things in your own best interests?

Do you often feel as though you can't be bothered to do the things you know are right?

Are you more interested in looking at problems or at finding solutions?

Do you treat people as you would wish to be treated, regardless of whether that person is valuable to you or not?

Do you see humility as a weakness?

Do you try to learn things from positive and less positive situations?

Do you have the ability to reflect on your past actions?

Who are the people you associate most with and how would they answer these questions?

What do you feel really strongly about?

In which areas of your life do you find it most difficult to be objective?

Where, and in what ways are you biased?

Where are your blind spots?

The above questions, when answered honestly and thoroughly analysed, should get you looking at your attitude, and be helpful in determining the things you may need to work on as soon as possible.

If you are beginning to get fed up with me talking about attitude and a positive state of mind, then I figure I am doing a good and necessary job.

Attitude is everything. Your attitude determines your thoughts, your thoughts determine your feelings, your feelings determine your actions and your actions determine your behaviour and your behaviour determines your results.

Earl Nightingale, who has been referred to as the 'Dean of Personal Development,' said this about attitude: "It is our actions, feelings, or moods, which determine the actions, feelings, or moods of others towards us, and which control to a surprising extent our success or failure. It is then, our attitude towards life which will determine life's attitude towards us."

If you're going to pass a test, present well at interview, or perform really well at court or any other task, it is your attitude or frame of mind that's key to your success.

So, if you're sure I am overstating the importance of a good attitude, I am very certain that it is exactly what you need to develop further.

The vital point to keep at the front of your mind is that giving evidence at court is very exposing because you are being scrutinised perpetually and your attitude is as unmistakable as a flashing beacon in the dark of night. It is instantly recognisable and a good attitude is every bit as conspicuous as a bad one. So, if your aim is to ensure you are seen in a positive light, then choose to have a good attitude. The court can't help but see it.

Before moving on from addressing your mind, to giving evidence at court, there is one more skill or ability you will need to master.

At this point you are probably thinking: "One more? Haven't I got enough to contend with already?"

And this is where I would reply: "I didn't at any time say being able to give good evidence at court was easy. If it was, there would be no need for this book, because anyone could do it without the benefit of help or support."

The skill or ability I am referring to, is the skill of mastering detail and organising that detail in your mind.

Key Learning Points.

- You have to know yourself or become self-aware to give a good account of yourself in the witness box.
- Get used to monitoring your thoughts and feelings, as it is a vital step in developing self-control.
- The key lies in being aware of your dominant emotional state and creating habits which develop and maintain a positive mental attitude.
- If you find you are lacking in any area, you have the capacity to begin to rectify your shortcoming immediately.
- If you are irascible you can become serene. If you are garrulous, you can learn to listen. If you are inclined to be thoughtless, you can develop consideration. If you are impolite, you can begin to behave courteously.
- You do not have to continue on a path that is not serving you. You can choose right now a state of mind that serves you and your child best.

Mastery Of Detail

"In the future, the great division will be between those who have trained themselves to handle these complexities and those who are overwhelmed by them - - those who can acquire skills and discipline their minds and those who are irrevocably distracted by all the media around them and can never focus enough to learn."

Robert Greene, Mastery.

If you are going to learn to give evidence adequately at court as a parent in either a private law matter or a public law matter, and certainly as a social worker, you will undoubtedly need to learn to master the details of your case.

This necessarily requires that you read and digest the court bundle or all the information placed before the court related to your family law case.

Now, I know this entails a lot of reading and organising this information in a manner that makes sense to you, or places it in order in your mind, but there's really no way around this. You have to know and understand all the pieces of information that are placed before the court, in order to know enough to effectively provide the court with convincing evidence.

Think of it this way, somewhere hidden within the pile of documents, may be pearls of information favourable to you, or minefields waiting to be unwittingly stepped upon at your peril simply because you didn't prioritise reading them.

Can you afford to neglect to apprise yourself of such critical pieces of information?

If you have taken any notice of what I have been saying throughout this book, you will know the obvious answer to that question.

You may recall, much earlier in the book, that I talked about lawyers taking painstaking effort to know the case fully. This is the job they do day in and day out for their living. What's at stake for them is whether they win the case or not.

It's clearly important for them, but it's just one case of many that they deal with.

In stark contrast, for you, this is your life, and the life of your child. So the stakes are, I believe, far higher for you and therefore it is imperative that you know all that there is to know about your case.

As a social worker, you also have to be aware that just one piece of information that you overlooked could be the difference between safeguarding a child, on the one hand, or failing to recognise that the child could remain at home with or without support, on the other.

Of course, it is normally more than one bit of evidence that a case turns on but some bits of evidence are more crucial than others and it may just be that the case pivots, on your detailed knowledge of the evidence.

You will no doubt have heard of the idiom, 'the devil is in the detail.' It is a phrase which means that mistakes are usually made in the small details of any undertaking. It is cautionary advice to pay attention to details, to avoid failure or delays with regard to progress.

I have found that things are seldom, as they seem to be. You and I are complex human beings, we are rarely straight forward people who behave logically. Instead, we are people who are motivated by our emotions to act in accordance with our strongest feelings.

Often if you study the details of a case diligently enough, you will begin to note a pattern of behaviour that repeats itself over and over again. These patterns of behaviour are a clear indicator of future behaviour, unless the person concerned has made a concerted effort, such as attending therapy to alter his or her actions.

For instance, the mother who can't help but fall into one relationship after another with men who abuse her. Or the father who has a chronic alcohol and anger management problem and displays it repeatedly with devastating impact.

Sometimes the pattern is conspicuous, to the point of it being obvious, at other times however, you will have to really study the history of events to gain a clear picture of what is occurring, in order to formulate an argument consistent with the evidence in the case.

We are creatures of habit, so if you observe someone long enough, even if they seek to conceal their 'disguised compliance' or undercover activities, their continued or repeated actions will become evident.

When reading a court bundle, take a pen and note down matters such as how many domestic disturbances occurred, how many of these the children observed, how often the children spent time with various other carers, how frequently children did not attend school, or parents were late to collect them, how many health appointments were missed over a period of time or how frequently contact with their children was missed.

It is equally important when making note of these statistics to discover the parent's stated reasons or claims for why these notable events have happened. If you keep searching for the real answers you will find them but you will need to keep an open mind throughout your exploration.

Sometimes you may find good or understandable reasons for recurring events that you as a social worker may be able to help with. At other times you may find that the parent's claim is nothing more than an elaborate (or less than elaborate) smokescreen, designed to distract and confuse you.

Here, your attention to detail and willingness to keep an accurate record of events including where necessary, a timeline of events, will be critical. Your attention to detail and mastery of these details will set you apart from other witnesses.

Recognise also, that we all have foibles and idiosyncratic or distinctive parts to our character which make us unique. These quirks of character need to be taken into account when seeking to understand and form sound conclusions about matters such as a parent's future behaviour, willingness to cooperate with professionals, place their child's needs before their own or keep their child safe from harm.

Whether you are a parent or a social worker, your capacity to master details, explore and think through the implications and consequences of these patterns and deftly incorporate them into your analysis, will unquestionably raise the quality and perception of your evidence.

I urge you to consider that the decisions that judges make are only as good or as bad as the information or evidence that is put before them.

It is your job to sift through the entire court bundle of evidence and find those crucial gems of information which point, like directions on a map, to an overall conclusion that is in the best interests of your child, or the child you are the allocated social worker for.

You can only do so when you master the details of the evidence before the court and organise those details in a coherent manner such that they can be easily conveyed, and from which sensible conclusions can be readily drawn.

Key Learning Points

- Read and digest all the information before the court – all the statements, reports, documents, exhibits, emails and letters.
- Lawyers or advocates painstakingly study each bit of information or evidence when preparing their case. You cannot afford to be any less diligent. Indeed, you need to be more so!
- Serious scrutiny of the evidence may yield a pattern of habitual behaviour which is vital to the outcome of the case.
- Make notes on salient matters or events impacting on the children and make use of statistics to strengthen your argument/s.

- Go about your preparation doggedly, but try to keep an open mind throughout your exploration of the evidence.
- Construct or use a timeline of events, as this may prove helpful to you.
- We are all creatures of habit and have idiosyncrasies which make our character distinct from others.
- Your job is to trawl through the evidence and find the gems of information which point to a conclusion about what's in the best interests of your child, or the child you are working with.

Giving Evidence In Court

"I agree with Scott Turow: A courtroom is inherently dramatic. You walk into court – it's like an ER, you know? Life and death is going on there. And it's moment-by-moment, and it's packed with energy. And even though you think you know what a witness is going to say, you can be wrong. Witnesses surprise you."

Marcia Clark

Prior to attending court, prepare the documents you need before-hand, ensuring that you have sent copies of your statement and relevant documents to the court and the parties at the court instructed times or dates.

You should make several copies of your court statement including any exhibits, one copy for the judge and others for the other party, or parties in the case.

When you are due to attend your court hearing, always be prepared to set out early from home, having planned your route in advance and taken the time to bring with you all the documents that you will need or may need on the day.

You will want to ensure you arrive at court early. If your court hearing is due to commence at 10.00, make sure you are at court at least 30 or 40 minutes before that time.

Attending court is already stressful enough, you do not need to be late and flustered and having to rush around.

Carry a pen and a note book, or diary if you use one, and always dress smartly for court. By smartly, I simply mean look clean, tidy and wear clothes appropriate for the court. What do I mean by this?

If you are a woman you could wear a suit, or a blouse, jacket and a skirt that you might wear to a formal event or gathering, or to an interview. I would advise against wearing any clothes that may be considered skimpy or scant. You want to positively influence or make a good impression on the judge via your attitude, sound judgement, behaviour and cogent evidence.

Wearing clothes that may be considered appropriate, in a bar or night club are unlikely to provide the court with the type of impression you want to make.

If you are a male, again you should dress formally. You may, or may not, wish to wear a shirt, suit and tie, but a shirt, trousers and a jacket at least, would be appropriate.

You would be well advised to wear shoes, not trainers, jeans, a cap or a hoodie.

This is my advice. The choice is of course all yours!

I learned a long time ago that we live in a world where people judge you without even being aware that they are doing so. Judges are human beings just like the rest of us and we all have biases.

I am thus suggesting you wear clothes suitable, or appropriate to attending court, it is perhaps a smaller issue than others discussed, but overall I think you will want to provide the court with a congruent image of who you are.

When you arrive at court, you will have to go through the court security process, where you will be asked to place your wallet or purse, any coins, mobiles, tablet laptops, devices or metal objects, into a tray.

You will then walk through a machine which detects whether you have any metallic objects which you missed or omitted to place in the tray. Once you have collected your possessions, you will need to find the court you are attending. Here it will help, if you have the case number to hand, which is a number the court uses to identify your case. It is normally found at the top of the page, towards the right hand corner of most court documents, just below the name of the court.

Just so that you are aware, if you have not been to court before, there is no guarantee how long you may have to wait outside of the court before being called in.

Be prepared to wait for several hours to get into court. Sometimes you may not get into court that day and another time and date will have to be scheduled.

This is a common experience that you will become familiar with if you have to attend court regularly.

Now you know that you may have to spend a lot of time waiting at court, you may want to bring someone with you who can wait with you outside of court, as well as a book or something to help occupy your time.

If you are called to give evidence in a private family law case, it is most likely to occur at either a Fact-finding Hearing or a Final Hearing.

When you get into court and are asked to commence giving your evidence, you will be ushered or shown into the witness box, which is situated close to the judge.

You will be asked by the court clerk whether you wish to take the oath, or to affirm. Depending on your religious persuasion, or lack of it, you will have the option of deciding which of the two is applicable to you.

As someone who was brought up within the Christian faith, I always take the oath, but there are no different expectations or higher values awarded to one over the other. Irrespective of whether you affirm or take the oath, you are required to give the court honest, truthful evidence.

Assuming you decide to take the oath, you will then be handed a Bible by the court clerk and asked to hold it in your right hand so it is visible to those in the courtroom. In your left hand the clerk will place a card and ask you to read the words on it. The words on the card are as follows: "I swear by Almighty God that the evidence I shall give, shall be the truth, the whole truth and nothing but the truth."

If you choose to affirm, the procedure is the same except, that you will repeat the following: "I do solemnly sincerely and truly declare and affirm that the evidence I shall give, shall be the truth, the whole truth and nothing but the truth."

A solicitor I once worked with referred to the experience of giving evidence as - you being placed in the 'hot box.' Another solicitor I worked with told me, just before I was due to go into the witness box: "I will open your evidence by asking you a few, brief questions... and then I will leave you to the wolves."

I mention this because I want you to realise, that these are not just interesting, colourful phrases that these solicitors have just plucked out of the air. They know only too well what awaits you in the witness box; they should know, they grill people like you and me all the time.

Consider also that I was not totally inexperienced at the time that these comments were made to me. I was a social work professional with several years of experience behind me.

How much more disadvantaged, do you think you, as a lay person are when placed in the witness box, on your own, up against voracious "wolves?"

Is it really any wonder why most people, and even a good many social workers and other professionals who have prepared to give evidence, leave court feeling savaged!

The comments by these lawyers should provide you with the motivation you need to prepare thoroughly.

Before I go into court, even now after the best part of thirty years of giving evidence at court, I still psych myself up for the experience of giving evidence and see myself sitting as comfortably as possible in the witness seat.

Only you know how you best get yourself into the calm, focused state of mind that you need to get into, but my advice is to mentally prepare and rehearse doing so over and over and over again. You should actually repeat the actions you take to put you in a good state of mind and to keep you in the mental attitude you need to remain in, so frequently that it becomes normal to you.

Your time in the witness box will be divided between your time answering questions from your advocate or lawyer and your time being cross-examined. You can expect to spend much more time being cross-examined than giving your evidence-in-chief, since that is your opponent's or, (in the case of a public law case) the other party's, opportunity to grill you with questions designed to discredit your evidence or character and expose any inconsistencies and weaknesses within your case.

In public law cases, so as not to confuse you, the other parties will only grill you, with the most difficult questions if they are your opponents. If they are in agreement with you, they will ask questions in support of yours and their case. They may ask questions to help clarify matters (if they consider the evidence you have given is not clear, or there is any doubt in connection with it) which either supports their case, or refutes your opponent's claims or evidence.

In terms of the procedure related to you giving evidence, if you have a legal representative, he or she will open your evidence by asking you to give the court your full name and address. They will then direct your attention to your statement, or statements and ask you to confirm that the statement/s and signature/s on the documents are yours, that the dates are correct and whether the contents are true to the best of your knowledge and belief.

You will then be asked questions by your advocate or legal representative. The aim of these questions is to set out your case and confirm all the details and facts which you rely upon to support your case that are within your knowledge.

The questions your advocate asks you are what is termed, '**examination-in-chief**.'

During examination-in-chief, your advocate, as a general rule is not allowed to ask you any questions which are said to be leading. In other words, they are not allowed to ask you questions which encourage or prompt you to answer in a particular way, so as to provide an answer which contains the information your advocate wanted you to confirm.

They will then ask you questions which hopefully you will be able to answer in a manner which corroborates your case.

If you are representing yourself, in other words, if you have not instructed a family lawyer, you will be expected to give an opening statement. Assuming you will not have done so before, it would be wise to keep this brief and to the point or as factual as possible.

What I mean by being factual, is perhaps best explained by you identifying events that you and your ex-partner agree has happened. These are matters, events or incidences which are not in dispute. It will also be very important to highlight the areas where you and your ex-partner are in dispute, as these are the matters that the court will need to decide upon.

In order to provide the court with an opening statement which is factual, it will have been necessary to have digested the case fully and to be clear on the pertinent matters that need to be addressed.

This is your opportunity to give a succinct summing up of your case, explaining how it is supported by the evidence. Just so that you are clear, this is not your opportunity or time to give evidence. It is your opportunity to summarise your case and you should plan to do so calmly and with forethought.

After you finish answering your advocates questions, or providing the court with your opening statement, you will then be asked questions, by your ex-partner's advocate, and this is called '**cross-examination**.'

Of course, in your private law case, it may be that neither you, or your ex-partner are represented by a lawyer. In which case your ex-partner will ask you questions, usually designed to refute your evidence, and show how their evidence should be preferred by the court than yours. In this scenario you will also have to cross-examine, or ask your ex-partner questions, intended to highlight the errors or weaknesses of their case and the accuracy of yours.

No matter whether you are cross-examined by your ex-partner or your ex-partner's lawyer, you need to continue to manage the process in a self-controlled, courteous manner. The same applies to your behaviour in the event that you are cross-examining your ex-partner. You never score any points by being rude.

If you are involved in a public law case, immediately following you giving evidence-in-chief, you will be cross-examined first by the applicants or local authority lawyer or barrister. After the applicant's finish cross-examining you, the lawyers for the other party's will cross-examine you.

In order to try and make things as clear to you as possible, if your public law case involves five different parties, then after the local authority finish cross-examining you, there will be three other people who will cross-examine you.

You're now probably wondering why there would be so many parties involved in your public law case?

To reiterate, in your **private** law case there are only two parties, you and your ex-partner.

In **public** law cases, there will be you (the first or second respondent - the mother is normally the first respondent, the father - the second) there may be your ex-partner – the second respondent, and the local authority (known as the Applicants).

The Children's Guardian is another party, whose job it is to represent your child's wishes and views (they work with a solicitor) and the fifth party may be either your child, if their views differs from that of the Children's

Guardian, or if the case involves more than one child (half siblings) there may be another father involved.

Key learning Points

- Ensure that, if necessary, your statements and any exhibits to your statement have been sent to the court and other parties at the required time or date.
- Bring with you everything you will need, such as pens, notebook, diary, your statement etc.
- Wear appropriate clothing if you seek to be viewed as a credible witness.
- Giving evidence is very much a mental and emotional exercise. Decide for yourself, how best to psych yourself up, and practise doing so over and over again, until you begin to feel confident that you can do this. Then do it some more.
- If unrepresented in your private family law case, you will be asked to give an opening statement. Here you should stick to the facts i.e. matters not in dispute. Give a short summary of the case and outline the matters in dispute that you want the judge to decide upon.

Cross-Examination

"There's nothing wrong in celebrating the good things in our past. But memories, like witnesses, do not always tell the truth. We need to cross-examine them, recognising and accepting the inconsistencies and gaps in those that make us proud and happy as well as those that cause us pain." **-Stephanie Coontz**

Whether you are giving evidence-in-chief, or being cross examined, you should look at the judge, and direct your answers in response to the questions asked, to him or her.

So although you are being asked questions by the lawyers, or by your ex-partner, when answering, you should direct your attention to the judge, as it is most important that he or she hears what you have to say.

Do not bother to turn your attention from the person questioning you to the judge, and then back again. It is, I think, a good habit to simply keep your focus towards the judge, which will save you time and energy.

You do not have to look at the judge all the time as that may be distracting, but angle your face more in the judge's general direction. You do not have to look at the person cross-examining you. The important thing is that you hear them and respond to their questions when you are ready to.

When you start speaking, try to keep your voice up. You do not need to shout, but try to keep the tone of your voice at a consistent level.

This is where practising speaking at home, or prior to your court appearance will pay dividends.

It will be natural for your tone to lower, or become less distinct, whenever you are unclear or lack confidence. You will need to work on this, because it will become immediately obvious to anyone observing you when you are unsure and lack confidence in what you are saying.

This is something you will have to practise as often as you can until you become more confident. It is important to realise that the way you say things is every bit as important as what you say. What you say and the way you say it, have to be congruent.

When being asked questions you should always listen carefully and wait for them to finish the whole question before you respond. You may find you are inclined to jump in and answer a question before the person asking you the question has finished speaking. This is a mistake and you should refrain from doing so.

It is a mistake because you have not heard the full question and yet you have jumped in, and made an attempt to answer it. You need to wait and hear the entire question. Listen to it carefully, think about how to answer it as fully as you can and then answer it.

When you jump at answering a question, you are often guessing at the question you have been asked. You are doing yourself a disservice, because you have to allow yourself time, to listen to the full question, understand it, and then formulate a reasoned response.

Whenever I have found myself jumping in or rushing to answer a question, I realise I am not in full control of myself and it is a sign that I am allowing emotions or stress to get the better of me.

You have to be able to recognise your feelings and take charge of them. The last time I made that error, the judge actually stopped me and told me to wait until the lawyer had finished the question. Clearly in my anxiety to answer the question, I hadn't even fully realised that the person had not finished the question yet.

The point I want to get across to you is that when you are giving evidence, there is no benefit to you or anyone else, in rushing. When you rush, you tend to make mistakes, and are not really in control of yourself.

Get into the habit of taking things slowly and at a pace that you can control your thoughts and responses.

Speak slowly and clearly, so that the judge can hear you.

Using an analogy of being a car driver, (if you are one) try to reflect back to when you first began to learn to drive. What was likely to happen to you when you performed your actions in too much of a rush, without sufficient care and control of your vehicle?

Yes...it's obvious isn't it!

You would most likely crash the car and cause much damage to yourself and potentially other people, unless your driving instructor intervened to stop you from losing control of the car.

Well, that's what the judge did for me on that occasion. But you do not want the judge to have to do that for you. You want, and need to be in control of yourself all the way through, and giving evidence is very unfamiliar, so you have to take your time in order to do the best job you can for yourself and ultimately for your child.

Show poise, take the time to step back a little and think about the question and how best you should answer it.

I want to stress that there is no disadvantage to you in taking everything at your own pace.

Let me make the situation crystal clear to you, it is in your advantage to do things slower than you may feel inclined to do because that way, you are less likely to make mistakes and more likely to remain in control of yourself. You should never allow yourself to feel pushed or bullied into rushing.

Do not worry about going too slowly, the judge understands that it is a pressurised environment and simply wants you to be able to give your evidence as honestly and clearly as possible.

The judge knows that there is no point in you rushing, so don't do it. Resist the urge and see giving evidence as your opportunity to set the record straight and explain exactly what has been going on.

This applies also when you are directed to turn to look at information within the court bundle of documents. You may be asked to read a sentence or a paragraph on a particular page of a bundle. Take your time to find the page and paragraph, and read it and ensure you understand it, before answering. It is not helpful to your case to complain later that you did not understand the paragraph or the question you were being asked.

It takes time and self-control and it is stressful, but you will do yourself no favours, by either allowing yourself to be rushed or, as a result of your own stress level, trying to do things too hastily.

On occasions even though you have waited for the person asking you a question to finish, it may be that you do not understand the question. When this happens, there is no harm or disadvantage to you in asking them to please repeat the question.

I do this whenever I have not fully heard or understood the question. It is a useful tactic because it allows you time to listen and think, before responding.

If after doing so, the question is still unclear to you, it may be that the way the question was posed is unclear. In such situations, you can say that you do not understand the question and ask that they break it down or ask it in another way.

The judge may often intervene at such times, either by simplifying the question for you, or by asking the lawyer or person cross-examining you, to break the question down point by point, so that it is easier for you to manage and for the court to be clear with regard to your evidence.

There is every likelihood that you may be asked a question which requires a 'yes' or a 'no' answer, but you may feel reluctant to answer it truthfully because you fear that it may show you up in a bad light or unfavourably.

Under such circumstances, you should answer the question truthfully, but then go on if appropriate or relevant, to explain the full situation.

For example, your ex-partners lawyer may seek to call into question the accuracy of your account of a particular event or incident and then may say: "It's true to say you really don't like Ms X very much, do you?"

Having listened fully to the question, you may know that the true answer is 'yes.' But if you just say yes, you have answered the question, but may not have answered the question in its entirety because there may be good reasons for you disliking Ms X. that if you do not find a way to explain, may show you up in a less than positive light.

Your answer then could be something like this: "Yes, it's true I don't like Ms X much, but that's because of the way she treats our child, and then articulate how her treatment is harmful."

Make sure when you provide the reason for your dislike of Ms X that there is a good reason for it (in this case I have used the example of poor treatment to your child) and also that you have clear evidence to back up or support your assertions.

So, in the above mentioned scenario, you would need to be able to produce evidence to show that Ms X had mistreated, abused or neglected your child.

Another way you could answer the question posed, would be to respond by saying: "I don't like the way Ms X behaves..." and then go on to explain what it is about their behaviour that you do not like, making sure that your explanation is not only supported by the evidence, but shows her behaviour in a poor light, and is consistent with the tone or content of your evidence.

By saying that you don't like the way Ms X behaves, you are demonstrating your capacity to differentiate between Ms X and Ms X's behaviour. In doing this, you shine the spotlight or attention on to Ms X's behaviour, and indicate that rather than having a blind loathing for Ms X, it is more of an understandable response to her treatment of the child you both produced.

It may seem like a small point, to you but you should also display in your evidence an acknowledgement that your son or daughter is yours and your ex-partner's child. So when you talk about him or her, on occasion refer to them as 'our' child.

This may be a small and obvious point to you but it helps depict you in a more reasonable light. So many parents going through their private and public family court case, due to acrimonious feelings, are loathe to refer to their child as a product of both parents.

What I would like you to contemplate is, how you would feel if you were your child?

If, as parents you have antipathy towards each other, how can your child fail to see it, how can he fail to be influenced by it, and ultimately, how can he or she possibly not be harmed by it?

When answering questions asked of you, always try to be polite, even if you believe the lawyer or your ex-partner is being unpleasant to you.

There will probably be times when you feel like arguing with the person cross-examining you. You must resist this temptation at all costs. Where necessary, politely disagree and explain why you disagree with whatever they are saying or arguing.

Being drawn into, or getting into an argument will, in no way serve your interests at court. It will instead indicate to the judge your proclivity to argue and will not help present you in a more reasonable, positive light. What it may also do, is make it look like you have something to hide.

Do your best to avoid presenting in a defensive manner, and do not deny something you know to be true. As mentioned earlier, answer the question truthfully and if you need to qualify your answer by explaining the circumstances in greater detail, do so.

It is equally important to your credibility that you do not come across as evasive. Always do your best to just answer the question. If you behave in a way that indicates evasion, then you effectively draw attention to your evasiveness and again it makes it look as though you have something to hide. When you do this, you can expect the lawyer cross-examining you to behave like a 'dog with a bone.' They are highly likely to keep asking you questions focused on the point you are being evasive about and in this way you place much more pressure on yourself.

In stark contrast, if you had simply told the truth, the lawyer would have moved on to the next point or question and even if giving the truthful answer immediately appeared unfavourable to you, at least the judge would see you as being honest.

Being seen as honest is very positive and a helpful step to being viewed as a credible witness.

Try to treat each question in the same way, in other words, afford it the same level of respect. Do not assume that every question is designed to trip you up or make you look silly or unreasonable.

Giving evidence and being cross-examined can be lengthy and tiring. If you feel your energy waning or you need to take a break to use the toilet, or just to revive your flagging energy levels, inform the judge.

If your throat becomes hoarse or you just need some water, there will almost always be a jug with water and plastic cups on the witness desk which you can use if you need it.

The nature of your court case involves conflict and difference of opinion. You will see things one way and your ex-partner or the local authority (in public law proceedings) will see things in a different way.

You may be asked, due to your difference of opinion, whether you consider the person or person's against you are lying or are being dishonest.

Here is where you should think carefully before answering. Even if you are one hundred percent sure that the person opposing you has lied, I would not advise you to call them a liar.

I would advise you to let the evidence speak for itself. Instead of calling your ex-partner or your social worker a liar, make sure you have clear evidence which supports your argument or account of what occurred.

For example, suppose you are having difficulty in being able to have contact or spend time with your child and that on numerous occasions the mother fails to pick up the phone or respond to text or emails you send to her.

At court her lawyer paints a picture of you of failing to keep contact with your child and suggests that your child is not bothered if, she sees you due to the amount of contact you have missed.

You dispute both the mother's account of failing to keep contact and that your daughter is no longer bothered about seeing you.

Her lawyer then says: "Are you accusing Ms X of lying?"

At this point you probably feel a strong urge to say 'yes.'

But I would suggest that instead of doing so, you show or demonstrate to the court the many dates you have tried to contact the mother, via phone, text and email, that have not been answered, resulting in you not seeing your daughter.

It is vital that you produce evidence via phone records, transcribed text messages and photocopied or scanned emails, of all these dates and times.

In addition, you might have written evidence, texts or video evidence, of your daughter expressing her desire to see you.

What I am indicating to you, is that showing the court this evidence or directing the court to such evidence, is the most powerful way to deal with this matter.

Your response then to the question could be similar to the following: "I cannot say for sure, as I am not her. But I seek to direct the courts attention to the exhibits shown with my written evidence (statement) which supports what I am saying."

Or you could say: "I am not calling her a liar. But the evidence on numerous occasions supports the view I have given. Any failure on my part to keep contact with my daughter relates solely to the dates I have been unable to get a response from Ms X."

Her lawyer may then try to repeat the question to get you to say, 'yes' you think s/he is a liar because that would likely be consistent with the story they wish to paint about you.

Here, you should stick to the response, you have already given, even if you can think of lots of times, in your opinion, when s/he has lied.

Simply respond by saying: “I have already answered your question, in the way I wish to answer it.”

Whenever possible avoid responding in the way their lawyer wants you to, or in a way that presents you as being confrontational and/or acrimonious.

It is much more powerful to let the evidence speak for itself and let the judge arrive at their own opinion or come to their own conclusion.

In this way, you present as someone who is measured and balanced, as opposed to being someone who is inclined to readily make accusations. Your actions and behaviour speak for themselves when you behave in this manner. You do not have to stress that they are lying and that you are telling the truth, since your behaviour demonstrates your character and the evidence can speak for itself.

But what if you were wrong about how you behaved about something and this is being brought up by your ex-partner or a lawyer and you are now being asked to comment on the issue.

Provided that you have thought the matter through and now fully understand where you may have gone wrong before, you should then acknowledge that you were not correct in your actions at that time and explain the way you thought in the past and how you have changed.

There is never anything wrong with acknowledging your own faults and shortcomings, the problem with most people is that they rarely do so, but are quick to point out the errors or flaws of others.

Perhaps it is becoming clear to you why I have spent quite a lot of time talking about parenting and taking the time to fully know your case. To ensure your behaviour is consistent with what is in your child's best interests and congruent with the arguments you make throughout your case.

If you have taken the time to do so, you are very unlikely to get caught out by behaviour which exposes you in an unfavourable light, without at least being aware of it and being able to show that you recognise any shortcomings and have made the necessary changes.

On this matter of behaviour which is harmful to your child and thus your case, whether past or current, although it should, I think, be absolutely clear by now, it is, and will always, be hugely damaging to your child to use them as a 'weapon' against the other parent.

If you think back for just a moment to what I was saying about how sensitive your child is and how much your children idolise and hero-worship their parents, you will know immediately how harmful this is to them.

Failing to recognise this as being incredibly harmful, would demonstrate a real shortcoming in your capacity to show empathy to your child.

A further matter you will need to bear in mind, is how vital it is for you to read, digest and understand all the information before the court. If your evidence makes reference to other statements, exhibits, or other pieces of evidence, make sure you have read and thoroughly understood everything in the other statement or evidence.

You can afford to leave no stone unturned and nothing to chance when preparing to give your evidence.

Lawyers undertake painstaking preparation before cross-examining you. Do you really think you can afford to be any less diligent or thorough when you prepare to give your evidence?

Something that might help you when preparing your evidence, is to produce a timeline of events so that you have a clear sense of the order in which events occurred. It is very helpful to you to know the dates when certain incidents, events, allegations, arguments etc. took place.

As the saying goes; "the devil is in the detail," and this is where you can easily be tripped up, confused or made to look incompetent or worse still, a liar.

Generally, during your everyday life, you do not need to keep a record of dates and times. These matters are often irrelevant to you because it's not the type of information you tend to keep in your mind, unless something conspicuous occurs, giving you a reason for a date or time to stick out in your mind.

However, when it comes to your written and verbal evidence in court, the more detail you can recall the better.

It is easy for a lawyer to make you look like a liar or to reduce the effectiveness of your evidence if you cannot remember dates or significant times when giving evidence. The more detailed and clear your evidence is, the better and more believable it will appear to be.

One of the traps parents, professionals and even experts can fall into, is being scared of coping with periods of silence when being cross-examined.

Lawyers are very astute, in that they are very aware of how uncomfortable most people feel when the weapon of silence is employed. They know that even though you may have answered their question, that just by them going silent, you may feel a strong urge to fill the silence by saying more.

Silence then is often effectively used to make you uncomfortable and unnerve you. When you volunteer more information, you invariably have lost self-control, you are responding in a knee-jerk manner and thus are likely to say something that has not been thought through in advance.

If you listen very carefully to the question and, as I have said earlier, think about how you wish to answer it, before answering it, there is then no need to feel that you have to say more.

If you wish to say more because you feel sure you can answer the question better, then that is fine because you have chosen whilst in full control of your emotions, to add to your answer. This is very different from letting unprepared words spill uncontrollably from your lips due to anxiety and discomfort.

Even if you do not end up damaging your case by saying something harmful, you will have exposed yourself as someone lacking control of your emotions and with a propensity to drivel on, rather than speak concisely.

It should be clear to you, that all of your answers and responses to questions fired at you by the person cross-examining you, need to be consistently centred around what is in the best interests of your child.

This is another reason why I have stated that you have to firstly know what's in your child's best interests, you then have to take the time to listen to the question fully and formulate an answer which is both consistent with what is best for your child and with your arguments or evidence.

There should be no room in your evidence or whatever you have written or orally communicated, for inconsistency. The lawyer cross-examining you will not fail to highlight any inconsistency in your evidence and use it to expose any weaknesses in your case.

You have to be able to keep your child at the forefront of your thoughts all of the time. You have to be constantly vigilant regarding any situations which may pose harm to your child, as you will need to show your ability to act in ways that minimise any harmful or risky factors associated with their wellbeing, whilst actively promoting situations or factors which promote their health, safety, development and wellbeing.

One of the tactics that lawyers cross-examining you often use, is to identify a small event or incident, highlight it, and then paint a picture which seeks to either discredit you or your evidence in some way, or that promotes their client in a positive light.

Essentially, what they have done is taken a micro-view of the evidence and tried to build a case around it.

What you have to do in answering any questions posed to you, is to make it clear that they have chosen to highlight one, or a small number of issues, which may appear consistent with their case.

However, overall (in other words a macro-view) what you have to show, is that in the vast majority of incidents the situation was not as the cross-examiner is portraying it.

Or that the context of the circumstances does not support the story or argument they are trying to portray.

When your cross-examination ends, the judge will ask your lawyer whether they want to re-examine you. They will tend to do so if there are matters that have been left unclear from your evidence.

If there is no re-examination, it may be that the judge has a question or two for you before your experience of giving evidence is brought to an end and you, no doubt, are able at last, to breathe a huge sigh of relief and leave the witness box.

Key Learning Points

- Keep your voice up and be aware of your body language.
- Listen fully to the question before trying to answer it.
- There is no need to rush, take your time to listen, think and then when you are ready, answer the question.

- If you do not understand the question, ask for it to be repeated. Do not take a guess at the answer.
- Always answer truthfully. If you need to qualify your answer, or explain it better, do so.
- Be polite when answering questions and do not permit yourself to argue or lose your temper.
- If you feel tired or your energy is waning whilst giving evidence, you can ask the judge if it will be alright to take a short break.
- Avoid calling someone a liar unless you have very clear evidence to support your assertion.
- Acknowledge your faults or shortcomings and do not be afraid to admit when you are wrong.
- Do not be scared of periods of silence, or feel pressured to fill the silence with ill-considered responses.
- Your answers must be focused on your child's wellbeing and best interests.
- Maintain a macro view of your case and keep the context of events and incidents in mind.

Case Studies

"Japan's very interesting. Some people think it copies things. I don't think that anymore. I think what they do is reinvent things. They will get something that's already been invented and study it until they thoroughly understand it. In some cases, they understand it better than the original inventor."

Steve Jobs

I have been thinking about the best way I can help you to gain an understanding of how to manage being cross-examined and I think the best way for me to do so entails providing you with Case Studies that you can hopefully relate to, understand and learn from.

I have decided then, to provide you with three case studies, two addressing private law matters and one addressing cross-examination of a parent and a social worker in a public law case.

In each case the cross-examination will begin with a question (Q) and be followed by an answer (A).

CASE STUDY 1

Involves Ms A and Mr E.

Ms A and Mr E had, prior to separating, been cohabitating for 13 years. They had a daughter Y aged 5 at the time of separation.

Ms A ended the relationship taking Y with her and returning to her family home.

Mr E was initially allowed to have contact with Y for two days per week.

Shortly after being given 2 days contact, he asked to have 3 nights contact, stating that he wanted to be supportive towards Ms A by shouldering his responsibility.

Then he requested to care for Y for 4 nights per week, again stating that he wanted to be of assistance to Ms A in caring for Y.

Ms A had left Mr E one weekend, saying that she was going to her mother's for the weekend, but had secretly planned to leave without telling him, due to his controlling, abusive and manipulative behaviour.

She claimed that Mr E had at one time, stolen her mobile phone, contacted every male contact that was unknown to him and then later had returned the phone by placing it in Y's bag telling her manipulatively, that

Ms A had made the mistake of dropping a television remote control (as opposed to her mobile) into her bag.

However, she felt guilty after leaving him and despite her experience of his behaviour, hoped that they could work together and share the care of Y.

Ms A acceded to Mr E's request and allowed him to have Y 4 nights per week.

Some 6 months after doing so, he made two applications, one to the Child Support Agency, the other to the Family Court, stating that Ms A stopped him from having regular contact with Y, accusing her of being abusive and unreasonable to him and to Y.

He complained that he had been willing to attend mediation but that Ms A had initially said she would attend also but had later been unwilling to do so.

Mr E stated that he had tried to get in contact with Ms A on numerous occasions and had sent her copious letters and emails to try to work out their dispute, but that sadly Ms A had shown that she was not willing to answer his correspondence or come to a mutually satisfactory agreement regarding the arrangements for Y's care.

Mr E asserted that Y had been very distressed by Ms A's refusal to allow Y to have regular contact with him. He accused her of regularly seeking to provoke and argue with him whenever Y was in their company and stated that he had personally observed her having a mental breakdown on three previous occasions.

He stated that he was consequently worried about Y being left in Ms A's care, and that as a result he had felt compelled to initiate court proceedings and was now applying for her to reside with him and to spend time with her mother.

In terms of his proposal about the amount of time Y should spend with her mother, he considered that she could see her mother from Friday afternoon at 4.00 to Sunday 2.00 pm.

Mr E further alleged that on one of the rare occasions he had recently been allowed to have contact with Y, on the 5th February this year, that she had turned up some 45 minutes late with Y, had been hostile towards him and failed to supply him with the blue and brown pumps she needed due to her asthmatic condition.

Ms A, in response to Mr E's application, has stated that she considers it is in Y's best interests to live with her and spend time with her father. She proposed that Y sees her father twice per week, once over the weekend and once mid-week. During the weekend, she proposed that a family member be allowed to collect Y or receive her from the agreed collection point, because she wanted to spare Y the distress experienced when in both parents' company.

At court under cross-examination, the following types of questions were put to Ms A and underneath the questions are the types of answers that I consider would be helpful to her case:

Q. It's true that you had a long term relationship with Mr E, isn't it?

A. Yes.

Q. What was the length of the relationship?

A. About thirteen years

Q. And how would you describe your relationship with Mr E?

A. The first few years were okay. There were some good times, but after the first few years, things at home became more tense and unhappy, particularly after Y's birth. Things became quite difficult from then onwards.

Q. You've stated that Mr E was abusive to you. In what way?

A. On one occasion before Y's birth he physically assaulted me, by slapping me across my face. After Y's birth things got much worse. He would call me names such as 'bitch,' 'whore,' and 'slut' and he wanted to know where I was all the time. Things were alright if I did ...basically what I was told. But if I didn't, he would get angry and be very verbally abusive.

Q. You say he assaulted you. What evidence do you have to support your allegation?

A. I don't have any evidence that he slapped me. I didn't take pictures or anything like that.

Q. Did you ever alert the authorities?

A. No. I didn't.

Q. Why not?

A. Because immediately after he hit me, he said he was sorry and pleaded with me to forgive him. He said he'd been under a lot of pressure at work, that he had people's lives in his hands and that the responsibility had made him do something he regretted.

Q. Would not that have been a perfectly sensible step to have taken…I mean that is, since you claim he was that abusive to you?

A. At the time…I mean after he hit me, he was very apologetic. He said he was stressed and that he had snapped due to work pressures. He begged me to forgive him… given his remorse, it felt a bit harsh to report the incident to the police.

Q. I see. Erm, help me with this will you? What caused the altercation between you and Mr E on that occasion?

A. It wasn't an altercation. We had not been arguing prior to the incident. He'd just flipped all of a sudden…

as far as I recall, it was because I came home a bit later than he expected and was talking on the phone to a male.

Q. Mr E recalled that you were talking to an ex-partner, someone who you knew he did not like or respect…isn't that the case?

A. No it isn't. I wasn't speaking to an ex-partner at all.

Q. You're sure about that are you, Mr E is adamant that he is correct?

A. Yes, I am quite sure.

Q. So what you're telling me is that Mr E has got it all wrong, you weren't speaking to one of your ex-partners called Hugh?

A. Well…yes and no. Yes, he has got it wrong because I wasn't speaking to my ex-partner at the time. And no, because I was speaking to a Hugh, but not the Hugh he obviously thought I was speaking to. The Hugh I was speaking to is a cousin of mine.

Q. Was… Y present, during this alleged abuse?

A. No Y wasn't present during the physically abusive incident, as I said she wasn't born at the time. But she has often been present when Mr E has called me derogatory names.

Q. You said Y wasn't present during the alleged incident of physical abuse?

A. Yes, correct.

Q. So, she wouldn't know anything about it?

A. Yes that's right.

Q. So, perhaps you can help me with this, how did she come to hear about the incident?

A. I have...I can't answer that question. I don't know.

Q. Well, it's clear from Mr E's statement that she somehow knows about it. So, how do you think she heard about it?

A. As I said, I don't have the slightest clue.

Q. When the incident occurred, was there anyone else present other than you and Mr E, who witnessed it?

A. No.

Q. Ms A are you really telling this court that you have no idea how Y came to know of this incident?

A. Yes. I have given you the only answer I can give you.

Q. Well you see my problem with your answer is that apart from you, the only other person who could have told her about the incident is Mr E. How likely do you think it is that Mr E would have chosen to tell Y such information?

A. I'm not him. If I was to answer that question, I'd be speculating. I can only tell you what I know for definite to be true.

Q. Are you suggesting that Mr E told her about it? That's pretty unlikely don't you think?

A. I have already answered the question. I'm not suggesting anything.

Q. What reason would he have to tell Y about it. Isn't it much more likely that you told Y about it, to malign his character?

A. As I said, I am not Mr E. But it is not totally out of character, for him to behave manipulatively. If, he told Y about the incident, he would have known that it would appear more likely that the information came from me. He has behaved manipulatively in the past, I refer to the time when my phone somehow disappeared. He convinced Y that the phone was instead a remote control device.

Q. That is a very serious allegation you are making with regard to Mr E. What evidence, if any do you have to support it?

A. Well…Y initially told me that her father had my phone. It was only later that she stated that it must have been a remote control. Secondly, a few of my male friends said that they had been contacted, out of the blue, by someone asking them questions about me. Although the caller gave what is believed to be a false name, at least two of my friends believed it was him. As shown in Exhibit 1 and 2

Q. That's hardly conclusive evidence. For a start isn't it plausible that Y could have made a mistake, when she thought he had your phone?

A. I think it's highly unlikely. Y knows the difference between my mobile phone and a remote control. Which child of her age, in this day and age, would be confused in that way?

Q. I don't see how that's not possible. Do you?

A. Everything is possible, but knowing Y and knowing how interested in and knowledgeable children of today are about mobile phones, I think it is much less likely that she would have not known the difference immediately.

Q. We may have to agree to differ there. And with regard to your male friends, all we have are two brief statements, claiming that they think the caller sounded like Mr E…. as I say, hardly conclusive.

A. No. Not conclusive but the fact is my phone was missing, for some three days. It was discovered in Y's bag, following her return from her time spent with Mr E….and the calls to my friends occurred a few days later.

Q. Well…let's stick to the facts, shall we…you were cohabiting with him for 13 years…that's correct isn't it?

A. Yes.

Q. You say he was emotionally abusive, controlling and on one occasion assaulted you. That's correct isn't it? And yet, at no time did you ever call the police!

A. Yes…and I explained why.

Q. Well I put it to you Ms A that instead of him being abusive to you, it was the other way round. It was you who were abusive to him. Isn't that true?

A. No. There is no truth in that.

Q. Mr E says that it was you who often tried to provoke him, and were abusive to him in the presence of Y. He stated that you become aggressive and abusive especially, when you are close to having a breakdown. Isn't that the case?

A. No. it's not the case…and I have never had a mental breakdown.

Q. Mr E has witnessed you having at least three mental health breakdowns. Are you saying this is untrue?

A. Yes. I have never had a mental health breakdown and I have never behaved aggressively or abusively to Mr E at any time.

Q. I see…so it's your contention that you have never had a mental health breakdown and that you have always behaved perfectly towards him?

A. I have never said that I behave perfectly. I am just not someone who enjoys arguments...and yes that's correct, I have never had a mental breakdown.

Q. Would you mind turning to Bundle C Page 32…it's an email sent…I understand from you to your local mental health agency. Is that, or is it not, an email you sent from your email address asking…in fact pleading for help?

A. This email was never sent by me. The email address is an old one I used to use many years ago. I haven't used that email address for about ten years now.

Q. So, you're saying that someone else sent that email. That's what you want this court to believe, is it?

A. Firstly, I've never had a reason to send such an email. There is no record of me receiving any type of mental health service and since I didn't send the email, the only person who could have sent it…and who knew my password was Mr E.

Q. I see, so now you're accusing Mr E of deliberately pretending to be you and sending a false email to your local mental health service? What reason would he have to do such a thing?

A. I have already mentioned that Mr E is someone who can be manipulative and when he chooses, has no problem with twisting the truth to suit his own purposes. For example, he has stated that I have had three mental health breakdowns. But there is no evidence of my involvement with any mental health services...except for this single email that I never wrote. If I'd had three mental health breakdowns, I'm sure there would be some evidence to verify or corroborate his claims.

Q. You don't really like or have any respect for Mr E. Do you?

A. ...He's the father of my daughter and always will be. We had some good times together. But I don't like the way he behaves, particularly when he abuses me in Y's presence. She doesn't deserve that. The thing is, this isn't happening by chance. It's by design. His design... and that's why I don't want to give him any further chances of exposing Y to his hatred of me.

Q. His hatred of you...I think Mr E would assert that it is the other way around...and with some justification.

A. I don't hate Mr E. I was in a relationship with him for a long time and he's Y's father, but I can't stand by and allow him to harm her because of his hatred for me. I'm not the person making a lot of allegations and applying to the court. He is.

Q. But you're the one seeking to cut down his contact with Y from 4 times per week to twice per week. He's just trying to protect his relationship with his daughter, can't you see that?

A. If that was what he was doing, there would have been no need to abuse me in front of Y, there would have been no need to go to court and there would have been no need to try to manipulate Y, or make up allegations such as mental health breakdowns for which there is no evidence.

Q. So what you'd have the court believe is that you've never been hostile to him or done anything which is intended to incense him? That's what you appear to be saying?

A. Yes, that's true.

Q. Well, let's look at a contact handover which occurred on the 5th February this year. It's right that you were some 45 minutes late to drop Y to her father, isn't that correct?

A. No it's incorrect. I set out on time. He knew that, because he was sending me angry, abusive messages whilst we were travelling and I told him that we were pretty much on time. My sister was driving us, so I was able to reply to one of his many abusive texts as shown at Exhibit 3.

When we arrived, he was nowhere to be seen and Y wanted a McDonalds Happy Meal, so we got in the queue whilst waiting. He appeared some 5 minutes later, some 6 or 7 minutes after the time we were due to meet and immediately began shouting and criticising me in front of Y and other people.

Y was so embarrassed and upset that she told me she didn't want to wait for her Happy Meal and just went to her father to appease and quieten him down. But that didn't stop him shouting at me some more before he left the restaurant.

Q. Your account is totally denied by my client. He maintains that you were both late and abusive to him. What do you say to that?

A. If he really cared about Y he wouldn't send the numerous abusive texts he does. The angry texts were sent before the meeting time. Neither would he be abusive to me, especially in her presence.

If it was really true that I had experienced three mental health breakdowns, how is sending me numerous abusive text messages, demonstrating his desire to protect his relationship with Y?

Q. Mr E accepts that he was a little annoyed but says that this was because you had often failed to give Y the medication she needed for her asthmatic condition. He believes you have a cavalier attitude towards Y's health. Isn't it true that you have failed to keep important health appointments for Y?

A. It is true I missed one appointment only because I didn't receive the letter. But this occurred when we were living together and the appointments are addressed to the parents of Y. So, it would be true to say we both missed that appointment.

Q. Who tends to take Y to her health appointments, you or Mr E?

A. It would be true to say Mr E takes Y to appointments related to asthma. But overall I take her to the vast majority of the health, and other appointments that she needs.

Q. Mr E would point out he has a very busy, responsible job, which takes up all of his time. But he makes a special effort when it comes to Y's asthma, because of the potential for it to be life-threatening. Wouldn't you agree that this should be prioritised?

A. To be honest, I am not sure to what extent, if at all, Y suffers from Asthma. I have never seen her have an asthma attack. On the other hand, I have seen him whip her up to such a state of anxiety, that as a result she probably has found it hard to breathe. As far as I am concerned, all her appointments are important…and my job is demanding also.

Q. So you don't believe she has asthma?

A. I have no conclusive evidence that she does. But Mr E has decided that she has asthma and has accused me of not taking her health seriously.

Q. I'm astonished. Isn't the truth of the matter, that you are so self-absorbed that you can't appreciate that Mr E is just appropriately concerned for his daughter's health?

A. I guess I would have to say, it's difficult to recognise Mr E's appropriate concern for our daughter, when he's engaged in making highly abusive remarks about me in Y's presence. I mean...it's hard to see that for an intelligent man, as he is, that he could fail to recognise, time and time again, that he was hurting Y when behaving in this way.

Q. Ms A once again you are making a very serious allegation against Mr E. Do you really expect the court to believe that he deliberately causes his daughter harm by behaving in the way you allege?

A. I can only give you my honest opinion and explain why I have come to the conclusion that I have.

Q. Very well...how would you describe Y's relationship with her father?

A. She loves him, he's her father. Under normal circumstances she likes to spend time with him. She wants his attention and to feel loved and worthy of love by him. I think Mr E doesn't always appreciate how much she wants his time and love. He is inclined to get her attention and excite her when he wants to, but at other times, it's as if he wants her to be seen and not heard.

Q. So, you acknowledge that she wants to spend more time with her father...and that she wants to feel loved by him?

A. Yes.

Q. And yet you seek to reduce the amount of time he can have with Y?

A. Yes, because I have realised that he isn't thinking about what's best for Y

Q. The same criticism could be directed at you, could it not?

A. I would love Y to have a better relationship with her father. I know it is one of the things she wants. But having looked at the way he has been behaving for the past 5 or so years, I have no reason to believe he will change in the way she needs him to.

Q. Y loves her father very much doesn't she?

A. I agree she loves him.

Q. Then why don't you facilitate the improvement that you say you want for Y's sake?

A. I would do if I believed it would really benefit their relationship. That's another reason why I allowed Mr E to have Y four nights per week.

Q. But you do recognise that Y is now used to seeing her father at least four times per week?

A. Yes, I recognise this, but he has not used the time to improve their relationship. He's used it to abuse me instead, and distress Y in the process.

Q. Ms A…I put it to you, that you're the one who is distressing Y, she wants to see her father regularly as she is used to.

A. I have never stopped Y from seeing her father, despite what Mr E claims in his statement. I agreed to allow him to see her 4 nights per week, hoping that he would show her the attention she wanted from him. But what did he do with that time? He used it to apply to the Child Support Agency, knowing that as a result of having her 4 nights per week that I would have to pay money to him, thus financially weakening me.

Yet he claims that I stopped him from seeing Y, when it is patently clear he was seeing her 4 nights per week. If this was not the case, then the Child Support agency would not have got involved. I certainly didn't contact them, as depicted in Exhibit 4.

Q. You have already accepted that Y loves her father, do you doubt that Mr E loves, Y?

A. I am not Mr E…to be honest, he has a funny way of showing it. And even if I agreed that he loves her, it doesn't mean that the way he chooses to show his love – by exposing her to conflict - is what would be best for Y.

Q. Do you seriously question Mr E's love for his daughter?

A. I can only go on his behaviour… I think if Mr E spent less time sending me copious abusive messages, making claims about me being mad and trying to financially destroy me, I would have less reason to see his behaviour as threatening to Y and myself.

End of cross-examination.

I hope the above has provided you with a clear idea of how to answer questions put to you under cross-examination. You will notice that the answers Ms A gave were measured and balanced. They were also backed up by Exhibits 1- 4.

Exhibits are evidence attached to your statement which support or show proof of the veracity of your statement or assertions. For the purpose of this case study, Exhibit1 and 2 were brief statements from male friends of Ms A, confirming being contacted by a man they believed was Mr E asking them about Ms A.

Exhibit 3 related to a number of transcribed abusive text messages from Mr E to Ms A on the 5th February handover. Exhibit 4 related to documentation from the Child Support Agency, proving that Ms A was required to pay money due to Mr E as she had the care of Y one day less per week than Mr E.

Where the questions simply called for a 'yes,' that answer was given. When the question required greater clarification or qualifying, the 'yes' would be followed by further information, to offer the judge a more rounded, macro-view of the circumstances, or context.

In this case study, which is from a real case, I have chosen to present only a very small portion of the evidence. Very often however, when you read all the evidence, you will be able to identify patterns, or recurring types of behaviour which provide you with evidence which you would be wise to analyse and make use of when giving your evidence.

The pattern may be that your ex-partner's evidence illustrates his or her propensity to lie or make claims that cannot be verified. Or it might be that he or she has a tendency, to provide evidence, which is inconsistent with other evidence.

Where you are able to point this out, it is very helpful to your case, providing it supports your basic argument/s, because then the evidence speaks for itself.

Your ex-partner only has to provide one clear lie, which when exposed demonstrates it may well be unwise for his or her evidence to be relied upon.

Obviously, these same points are equally relevant to you. So you need to ensure that you don't tell any untruths and that the evidence you present does not expose any patterns of behaviour that your ex-partner's lawyer can use against you.

This is why I have stressed the importance of you reading and knowing all the evidence before the court.

There were occasions when the lawyer tried to get Ms A to make statements that would portray her as unbalanced, acrimonious or unable to behave in ways consistent with Y's wellbeing.

Ms A's responses were well thought out. For example, the cross-examiner wanted her to call Mr E a liar. Ms A however did not directly do so. She side-stepped those traps by referring to the evidence, or choosing to answer in a way, that did not directly accuse her ex-partner of lying but simply cited the evidence, which exposed the inconsistency of his account.

Where she considered he was manipulative, she explained, or produced evidence to explain her reasoning or conclusions.

In my view this creates a far better presentation of both your character and the quality of evidence you provide.

Ms A was able to maintain her composure, answer the questions honestly and remain focused on whatever was in Y's best interests throughout her time giving evidence. Her ability to do so would have been compromised if she was not able to concentrate, listen very carefully to the questions asked of her and then take her time to think about providing answers that were consistent with the evidence and congruent with both Y's best interests and the arguments or proposals outlined in her case.

Now let's look at a different Case Study, and in order to assist your learning about the importance of providing verbal evidence which is consistent with your written evidence, I shall also provide a sample of a court statement below following the case study.

Case Study 2

Mr B and Ms C had been in a five year relationship and had been cohabiting for some 4 years.

They produced a child S who was coming up to 3 years when they separated, following Mr B ending their relationship and returning to live with family members right across the other side of the city.

Prior to the relationship coming to an end, Mr B and S had developed a really close bond of attachment. Shortly before the end of the relationship, Mr B had met another woman and had commenced a relationship with her.

The relationship between him and Ms C had been strained and volatile many months before it ended, but Mr B had been unwilling to end the relationship, because he feared losing contact with his daughter S.

He recalled telling Ms C several years earlier during better times in their relationship, that the last thing he would ever want to do, would be to have to go to court, due to them having a dispute about their care of S.

However, following their separation, all communication between him and Ms C broke down. Ms C blamed him for the demise of their relationship, was angry about him commencing a new relationship and for several months would either fail to return his calls or simply made it impossible for him to have contact with S.

During one phone call (at the beginning of May) in which Mr B was able to talk with Ms C, he asked to talk on the phone to S, but Ms C refused to allow him to, and then advised that he should get used to it, because she would not be spending any time with him.

After a few more weeks of denying Mr B contact with S, Ms C returned his call one day, and agreed to allow him to visit S, the following Wednesday 31st May at 2.00 pm.

On the day agreed, Mr B drove the 20-plus mile journey and arrived at the agreed address, where S and her mother Ms C were living. He arrived at 1.55 parked his car and pressed the doorbell.

Minutes passed, but no one answered the door. He returned to his car and then called her mobile. Again there was no answer, the line just kept ringing.

He decided to wait in his car as he had come all the way from home, and hadn't seen S for 3 months, and needed to know how she was. Eventually he pressed the bell again, and knocked on the door and this time Ms C answered it.

Immediately, she became abusive and Mr B, who was by now not in a good mood, reacted to her abuse, by arguing back with her. In the midst of their argument he saw S for a few moments before Ms C physically attacked him.

S began to cry and Mr B realised, that the best thing he could do was use any self-control he had left to walk out the door, before things got worse and S became more distraught. As he walked through the door he heard Ms C swearing at him, accusing him of abusing her, and saying that she was going to call the police to arrest him.

The police were called and they spoke to Mr B after speaking to Ms C. They did not arrest him, but advised him that he needed to speak to a solicitor.

Following this incident, Mr B did just that, and applied to the family court to spend time with his daughter S, proposing that he spent from Friday evening to Saturday evening every week.

Ms C's statement in response to Mr B's proposals, was that she would not agree to any overnight stays as she complained that Mr B was irresponsible and that S's needs would come a poor second to any woman he was seeing.

She further alleged that Mr B had been emotionally abusive to her and violent on a few occasions. She stated that S had observed these incidents and was traumatised and fearful of her father.

As a result, she was not willing to agree any contact, unless it was supervised and S protected from any harm she stated Mr B posed with regard to her.

Sample of Court or Witness Statement

IN THE FAMILY COURT SITTING AT......
(The name of the court)

AND IN THE MATTER OF THE CHILD:
S....B..... d.o.b. 20/6/17

Statement for the Applicant

Name of Applicant: Mr...... B.....

Statement No. 1

Date: 12/7/20

Case Number:
(this is the number given to your case by the court)

BETWEEN:	MR ..... B......	Applicant
	And	
	Ms ..... C......	Respondent

FIRST STATEMENT OF THE APPLICANT
MR ..... B.......

This statement has been written in support of my daughter S's need to have good quality regular contact with me, which has not occurred now for the past 5 months, following the breakdown of my relationship with S's mother – Ms C.

I met the respondent, Ms C in March of 2015 and commenced a relationship with her shortly afterwards. We dated for a year and then commenced cohabiting in the summer of 2016, when I moved into her home.

The first few years together were good and in June 2017 we were fortunate enough to produce our daughter S.

S was always a very bright bundle of joy and as I worked from home mostly, we spent a lot of time together and developed a really close relationship.

Although my relationship with Ms C was good at the beginning and for some time, our relationship began to deteriorate after S was born.

We began to argue as a result of having different priorities. Looking back now, I think it is true to say that she valued making our home look beautiful, whilst I valued working towards making our relationship more harmonious.

It was important to me that we were emotionally close, but we began drifting further and further apart. Our rows were becoming more heated and it was this reality and the fact that S would hear and observe our conflict, which compelled me to make a decision, I had been procrastinating about for many months.

Despite our numerous rows there were only two occasions in which our conflict escalated to physical violence. Unfortunately, on both of these occasions, I am sad to say, S was present.

The first occasion occurred at the end of February when we finally ended our relationship. On that occasion Ms C flew into a rage because our relationship was ending and she knew I had, a few weeks earlier, commenced a new relationship.

She physically attacked me, scratched me and tried to hit me. I did not retaliate, but did defend myself. This incident occurred also in the presence of one of Ms C's friends, who I urged at the time to take S elsewhere, so as to minimise her distress at seeing her parent's conflict.

The other occasion which led to physical violence occurred on the 31st May when I was at last allowed to see S at their home. Ms C had told me to arrive at her home at 2.00 pm, but when I rung her doorbell, there was no response for about fifteen to twenty minutes.

This was very frustrating and annoying for me, because I had driven the best part of twenty-plus miles to see S, who I had been prevented from seeing for 3 months.

When Ms C eventually opened the door to allow me entrance, she immediately began verbally cursing me. Unfortunately, I was still annoyed at her for making me wait and when I made the mistake of verbally responding in kind, she flew at me and again tried to hit, scratch and claw at me.

This occurred in the presence of S, once again, and as a result, although I desperately wanted to see her, I had to use all of my self-control to leave her property, to avoid S becoming more distressed.

Ms C called the police and alleged that I had physically assaulted her. The police spoke to me, after speaking to her. I was not charged. Instead, after listening to my account, they advised me to see a solicitor.

Going through the court process to gain contact with our daughter was something I was very reluctant to do. But during a phone conversation with Ms C, at the beginning of May, she told me that I had better get used to not seeing S because I was not going to be allowed to see much of her.

It was after her words and behaviour during the incident at the end of May, when she called the police, that I eventually made the decision to apply to the court for a Child Arrangement order.

Although Ms C called the police on me and has alleged that I have physically abused and assaulted her, this has never happened and there has never been any evidence to corroborate her allegations.

The reason I have taken the decision to apply to the court, is in the hope that I may be granted reasonable contact with my daughter. Since I ended my relationship with Ms C in February 2020, I have not been able to gain any contact with her, except for a very brief occasion in May, when Ms C called the police on me.

Virtually all my efforts to make contact with Ms C, in order to arrange spending time with S have been unsuccessful, as it has become extremely difficult to contact Ms C. When I have called her in the hope of arranging contact, it has not been possible to get through to her as her phone cuts off and there has been no facility to leave a voice message.

The only time I was able to get through to her, was at the beginning of May and this happened when I called her mobile from a private number. A few weeks later she responded and agreed to me visiting at the end of May. Since that time, my efforts to make contact with Ms C by phone, using a private line or otherwise, have not been successful. As a result, I have felt forced to apply to the family court.

My proposal is that contact between S and myself is resumed, as swiftly as possible. I would like to see her at least once per week.

My suggestion is that I be allowed to pick her up on Friday evenings and have her overnight until Saturday evening, at about 6.00 pm. That would be my preferred option, but I am open to seeing S during the week, or on Saturday night to Sunday evening, if that is considered more suitable by the court and Ms C

As stated earlier, S and I developed a great relationship prior to the break-up of my relationship with Ms C and I believe it is very much in her interest to resume her contact with me.

My relationship with Ms C is currently not a harmonious one. I hope this will change in the future.

If S is at her nursery on Fridays I would happily collect her from there, as I wish to avoid subjecting S to any further distress, and so would seek to limit coming into contact with Ms C, where possible. If this is not possible I will pick her up from home, or from any other suitable venue.

To reiterate, I am seeking a Child Arrangement order, which would enable S to spend reasonable quality time with me, on a regular basis. I would hope this would occur at least, on a weekly basis.

I, the applicant, BELIEVE THE FACTS STATED IN THIS STATEMENT ARE TRUE.

Signature ....

Name.................

Date

Mr B was asked the following questions during cross-examination and answered as follows:

Q. Mr B I'm asking you questions on behalf of Ms C. You've applied to the court to be able to spend time with your daughter, that's correct isn't it?

A. Yes.

Q. And…how old is S?

A. She's three.

Q .And…when was the last time you spent time with her?

A. …apart from seeing her a few moments in May…the last time I spent any time with her was 5 months ago.

Q. Five months is a long time to be away from your three-year old, wouldn't you agree?

A. Yes I would.

Q. So why were you?

A. Ms C wouldn't allow me to see her!

Q. Yes, you mention that in your statement, but exactly what efforts did you make to see S?

A. After we broke up, I recall contacting her on numerous occasions. I began calling her two weeks after we split-up. On one occasion…after the break-up, she answered my call. She refused to allow me to talk to S and threatened that I would not be seeing much of her.

Q. Ms C remembers that call, but states that she was just angry at the time. She expected that you would make the effort to ring back on other occasions, but says you didn't. What happened?

A. What happened was that I kept trying to contact her, but she never, apart from one occasion, answered my calls.

Q. Do you have a record of the dates you claim to have called her?

A. I can't recall all the exact dates from memory but I can remember some of them.

Q. Some dates…I see, what dates are those?

A.…the 15th March, 2nd May,1st June,14th June, 23rd June, the 2ndJuly, the 10thJuly.

Q. But, you broke up in February. Correct?

A. Yes.

Q. So…help me with this please, what happened between February and May?

A. I called her…at least twice a month in March, April and May, but she never responded.

Q. You say you called her, but you don't have the dates. Do you?

A. Not all of them, no.

Q. Well, forgive me but …anyone could say they called. Apart from the date in March and the date in May, can you identify any other date that you called within the first 3 months?

A. No. I can't, I've given you the dates I can remember.

Q. Help me with this, if you can…did you leave a voice message?

A. I would have done, if it had been possible to do so.

Q. What do you mean by that? Ms C's phone has the facility to accept voice messages.

A. I'm aware of that, but each time I called from my mobile (without withholding my number) the line went dead and there was no voicemail facility.

Q. Are you suggesting that Ms C saw your number and deliberately chose not to answer?

A. I can't be 100% sure, but when I called again I got the same response and when I think back now, I realise that the one time I got an answer from her, at the beginning of May, I called her from an unknown or private number.

Q. Ms C denies deliberately not answering your calls. Sounds to me like you're trying to shift the responsibility for your failure to recall the dates of the calls you say you made, onto Ms C. That's what you're trying to do isn't it?

A. No. I am just trying to answer your questions as honestly as I can.

Q. Mr B, the problem I think this court has with your evidence, is that frankly you have no evidence, do you? No evidence to confirm or corroborate the dates, you say you called.

A. I can't remember all the dates before May, but I could find them out from my phone provider's records.

Q. But, you expect this court to believe, you were desperate to spend time with your daughter, when you've neglected to bring all the evidence necessary to support your claims?

A. I remember the dates from May. Before that I didn't think about it, because I didn't want to go to court…and I didn't know I was going to have to go to court to be able to see my daughter.

…I guess if I had more experience of court, I would have thought about it more and got the evidence to prove what I'm saying.

Q. Well you see that's my client's case – that you didn't think about it. But in this case the 'it' was your three year old daughter S. Did you forget about her while you were otherwise occupied?

A. No I did not. When I said I didn't think about it, I was referring to not thinking about going to court. If I had have realised I was going to need every single date I called Ms C., then I could have got it…and I still can, if the court will allow me to file that evidence, albeit late.

Q. What you're saying is you didn't think you'd need all the evidence to prove your case? Are you seriously telling the court, that you did not think you'd need this evidence?

A. I've not been to court before. It might sound incredible to you, but it's not like I've been through this lots of times….I just want to spend reasonable time with S, and be a father to her.

Q. Very well, let me ask you this, by June you had not seen her for almost 4 months, why didn't you apply to the court sooner, if you were really that anxious to see S?

A. As I said in my statement, and as Ms C knows very well, I didn't want to take her to court. It's one of the last things I wanted to do, I hoped she'd let me see her, but after the phone call in early May, when she told me I wouldn't be seeing S much, and then her behaviour when she attacked me, and then called the police on me, she gave me no choice.

Q. Ms C acknowledges she said you wouldn't see her much, it was said in a moment of anger, but it seemed plain to her, even then, that you were not that bothered about seeing S, isn't that the truth?

A. No, not at all. I miss her every day. I…I'm a quite a private person. I don't like that I have felt forced to involve people I don't know in my private, family affair. But I was left with no alternative. I don't know what the outcome will be …but I am sure that if I hadn't taken the case to court I probably wouldn't be seeing S until she was old enough to find me.

I…it's my responsibility to make contact to arrange to see S, but it doesn't seem to me, as though it matters at all to Ms C whether S sees me or not.

Q. Well she would say that you didn't show any desire to be part of S's life. She has no record of you making contact with her. Do you see?

A. No I don't. I made contact with her on at least 6 or 7 occasions that I can confirm via my mobile records. Yet only on one occasion did she see fit to get back to me… and when she did, she engineered a situation in which S would see physical violence, and which she used to call the police on me.

Q. Apart from your lack of interest in S. Ms C, also points to your abusive behaviour, as a reason she has shown reluctance to arrange times, for S to have time with you. What do you say to that?

A. I've never shown a lack of interest in S…and there was and never has been any truth, in her claim that I was abusive to her. Even when she called the police on me, there was no evidence then, or at any other time.

Q. But, you admit that S saw violence on that occasion. Did you forget that she was present?

A. S saw her mother attack me. I was angry, but I did not retaliate, I defended myself, I turned around and walked back through the door, because I was aware of S's presence and her distress.

Q. You seem to be laying all the blame at Ms C's door, but you acknowledge that you were not in a good mood, isn't that true?

A. It is true I wasn't in a good mood, yes, due to her making me wait so long to see S and then choosing not to answer her phone.

Q. Given that you were in a bad mood, is it possible that it was your attitude that played a crucial part, which led to the fracas between you and Ms C?

A. I acknowledge I wasn't in the best of moods, but I think it is highly unlikely because before I even opened my mouth, she began abusing me.

Q. She denies your claim and maintains that you were hostile from the start and more or less pushed past her and entered her property. This is what caused her to be angry at you, isn't that correct?

A. No, not at all. I would never just push past her and enter someone's house. She let me in, but began shouting at me the moment I entered her property. When I argued back, that's when she physically attacked me.

Q. Ms C has no recollection whatsoever of attacking you first. It's her contention that you got, as she says, 'in her face' and this led to the fracas. You acted threateningly and she responded didn't she?

A. That is not what happened at all. As I've said, before I said a word she began berating me. When I argued back she snapped and attacked me physically.

Q. Very well, we will have to agree to disagree on that point. But you do accept that you retaliated, arguing in S's presence.

A. Yes, I accept this. I was angry, but it was because of S's distress that I turned round, and walked back out of the door, as I had no desire to upset her.

Q. But you clearly did, didn't you?

A. I accept that we both upset her. It is something I very much regret, as she doesn't deserve to be exposed to that kind of behaviour, and it's something I intend to try to ensure never happens again.

Q. But, that wasn't the first time that S saw you fighting was it?

A. No.

Q. When else did she observe you fighting with her mother?

A. There were only two occasions when there was physical violence and on both those occasions Ms C attacked me…and unfortunately S was present both times.

Q. You say Ms C attacked you on both occasions. What role did you play in these alleged assaults, were you just an innocent bystander?

A. No. I wasn't an innocent bystander, but I did not initiate, at any time, physical violence. I am not seeking to present myself as perfect, there were things I wish I hadn't done or had done better, but I never wanted S to observe or be exposed to our conflict – that's one of the main reasons, I ended the relationship.

Q. What are the things you wish you hadn't done?

A. I…wish…there are a number of things. I wish we could have sorted out our problems, so that I never had to leave S in the first place.

I wish I could have left Ms C on better terms. I regret starting a new relationship shortly before ending our relationship.

I regret getting into arguments with Ms C at all, but especially when S was present.

I regret S being exposed to anything other than positive experiences.

Q. So, what you want the court to believe is that, all the violence was initiated by Ms C? That is what you're saying isn't it?

A. Yes. Essentially everything became an argument, and that was not what I wanted for S, or myself. So, I'm not saying that I didn't do things that upset or wound her up, obviously I did. But the willingness to argue and fight didn't come from me.

Q. You're painting a picture of yourself as someone who was focused on S's welfare and yet S was traumatised when she saw you hurting her mother, isn't that so?

A. I have already explained that this is not the case. I have no doubt she was traumatised by the incidents she saw, but at no time was I physically hurting her mother. I didn't do that.

Q. Well Ms C doesn't accept that at all. You're quite a large man...how tall are you 6 foot 2 or 3inches?

A. About 6 foot 2 inches.

Q. How much do you weigh...14, 15 stone?

A. 15 stone.

Q. And Ms C is...at best 5 feet 5 inches, that's correct isn't it?

A. About that, yes.

Q. So…when you got into a fight with her, from S's point of view, who was a quarter of her mother's size, can you see how traumatic that would have been for S to witness?

A. First of all I need to make this clear. I never fought with Ms C. I defended myself, which means that when she was trying to hit and scratch me, I held her off as best I could. I did not hit her or shove her.

Now, of course, I am much bigger than Ms C and we are both giants to S, and seeing this will have been very frightening for her, but at no time did she see me hit or physically harm her mother.

Q. You say you never fought with Ms C…well what would you call it?

A. …The distinction I am trying to explain to you is that, in the way I see it, a fight is when two people are physically trying to hurt each other. In this case Ms C was trying to hurt me, but I was not trying to hurt her, I was trying to get away from her and reduce S's distress.

Q. So you wouldn't call it a fight ok, but why do you think that S is scared of you?

A. I can't tell you what S may or may not have been exposed to when not in my care. What I can tell you is that whilst S was in my care, she was never frightened of me. We had developed a great relationship.

Q. Mmm, so you say....but Ms C says that since the violent incident in May, S is nervous, just at the mention of your name. You didn't know that did you?

A. No. All I can tell you is that she was never scared of me.

Q. Yes but that was several months ago, before...the recent incidents of violence. Do you understand that?

A. I understand what you're saying, but I find that very hard to believe.

Q. Well...you haven't been around for several months, so you wouldn't know would you?

A. No I haven't, and not from choice. If S is demonstrating any fear at the mention of my name, I would have to question what has been said to her, during the time I've not been allowed to see her.

Q. You're implying that Ms C has said or done, something to bring about this situation?

A. I can't think of any other reason why S would, allegedly, be fearful of the mere mention of my name, particularly when our relationship was a very positive one.

Q. That may have been the case, but I'm sure you recognise that things change. Incidents of fighting or violence can traumatise young children, and leave them scared as a result. So do you see that Ms C has had nothing to do with it?

A. I can't directly accuse her of anything…I don't even know if it's true, but if for any reason she is scared of me, all the more reason for her to see me, initially in a supervised environment, so that any potential reservations can be dispelled and our relationship be resumed.

Q. So you're in agreement with Ms C's proposals regarding contact?

A. I have my reservations about her account of S's feelings, but if it serves to put her mind at rest, and most importantly allows S to feel safe, and be allowed to see me, then I am happy to see her, as a starting point, under supervised conditions.

Q. Well, yes it would, she's listening to S and putting her needs first. Wouldn't you agree that's the appropriate thing to do?

A. My first priority is to ensure S is safe and secure from harm. My second priority and linked to the first, is to re-establish contact with her, see that she is ok and begin to play a positive role in her life. So, I'll comply with whatever makes that possible.

Q. You agree then that overnight stays at the moment are not appropriate given S's feelings and Ms C's related concerns?

A. My position, I will repeat, is that I have reservations about Ms C's claims that S is frightened of me. But in order to progress matters, I am prepared to agree to commence seeing S at a contact centre, if the court thinks that's the best way forward. Obviously, my preferred proposal is, as I have stated (i.e. overnight stay from Friday night to Saturday).

End of cross-examination.

One of the key learning points from Case Study 2 is the importance of attending court with all the supporting evidence you intend to rely on. It's of little use turning up at court as Mr B did, without the mobile telephone records to prove that he had made several calls to Ms C.

If Mr B had all the phone records, he would have been able to state that that he had made in excess of twelve calls to Ms C, and yet had received only one response. This would have been a very powerful, statistical piece of evidence to show the court.

You should be aware that the judge does not know you at all. He or she can only go on what your written and verbal evidence is and make a judgement about your character from that. So the more evidence you have which backs up what you are saying, the better for you.

What I have tried to demonstrate to you, when answering questions under cross-examination, is that it is important to answer the question, but remember that there are often many different ways to respond to a question asked of you.

For example, one of the questions Mr B was asked related to the incident when S witnessed a physical altercation between her parents, the question posed was, 'but you clearly did upset her didn't you?'

Mr B's response was, 'I accept that we both upset her. It is something I very much regret as she doesn't deserve to be exposed to that kind of behaviour and it's something I intend to try to ensure never happens again.'

The lawyer then was keen to portray a picture of Mr B upsetting S, which was true. Or to be more precise, it was partially true. It was partially true because both he and Ms C's physical altercation had distressed S.

So Mr B is acknowledging his part in upsetting S, but makes clear via his other responses that he was only defending himself. He then goes on to comment that he very much regretted exposing S to any type of behaviour that distresses her and continues on to make the court aware that he takes such incidents seriously and thus intends to ensure she is not exposed to such behaviour again.

Now, Mr B could have answered that question by saying that he did not consider that he upset S during that incident. He could have said, "I don't think S was upset as a result of my behaviour or actions," and could have gone on to place all the responsibility for S's distress on Ms C.

The reason I am suggesting that Mr B respond in the kind of way I have is because the purpose of his presentation is to come across as a father who understands and is empathic regarding S's feelings. So whilst Ms C was the person who physically attacked him and even though he did not physically retaliate, nevertheless S will have been left very upset by seeing her parents engaged in violence.

Mr B then is showing that he has insight into S's needs and can see things from her point of view.

Had Mr B remarked that he did not think S was upset, by witnessing incidents of violence, he would very likely have presented as a father who was not aware of how his young daughter would have experienced the incident.

If he had been solely concerned with showing that he was not the one to blame for the distressing incident, he would also have demonstrated, I think, a lack of balance and responsibility in addition.

You're probably now questioning why, if you were Mr B, you should accept the level of responsibility he assumed, given the role played by Ms C in initiating the abuse and violence?

But your aim is to present as someone the judge can see as able to be fair and focused first and foremost on S's wellbeing.

In my view, it is not in your interests to present as a parent who is more concerned with 'being right' and blaming Ms C, than demonstrating concern for S, who is at the mercy of her parents.

This is a really important point, which I hope you can grasp.

In this scenario Ms C has had most of the power, she has prevented Mr B from having contact and been abusive and violent, but you (if you are Mr B in such a scenario) have to prove to the court, that you are balanced and, most importantly, able to prioritise S's needs before those of your own.

If you are able to see things from S's viewpoint, you will realise she has done nothing to warrant exposure to this distressing incident and that if Ms C cannot, or will not protect her from witnessing such events, then you as Mr B have to be that much more attuned to S's needs for the court to be able to recognise your capacity in this regard.

Alternatively, Mr B could have answered, "Yeah, I upset her but that was only because Ms C wound me up in the first place, and then started having a go at me in front of her. If I hadn't been denied contact and Ms C had not, behaved in the way she did, S would not have been upset."

Although in this scenario Mr B shows some insight into S's feelings by accepting that he upset S, he then just goes on to blame Ms C again, which I consider would provide the court with little to suggest that he is appropriately focused on S's needs, and feelings and it's fairly clear that if Mr B thinks in this way that S is likely to continue being exposed to her parent's conflict in the future.

There is often a tendency for you, as a parent in conflict with your ex-partner, to be concerned with your ex-partner's behaviour. This should not be the focus of your concern. Your concern should always be on the best interests of your child and on how you are behaving and presenting at court

What I am encouraging you to do is, think strategically, concerning how you come across at court, since this is presumably your reason for reading this book.

However, like S, your child will need you to think in the ways I am suggesting, not just for the purposes of making a good impression, at court but more importantly in providing your child with the appropriate level of care that they need and deserve, if they are to grow up to become productive, healthy, independent adults.

I consider I would be doing you, and your child a disservice, if I did not make it clear that the principles I am suggesting you adopt are congruent not just with achieving the best outcome at court, but with offering your child the best care throughout their childhood and beyond.

One of the first questions put to Mr B, was a question about S's age.

How do you think he would have been seen by the court, had he not known her precise age?

In my view, it is very important to know your child's age. I consider that it shows the court, that you are thinking about them. It gives an impression that you take an active interest in your child's life.

Now, there may be other reasons why you as a parent do not or cannot remember your child's age. Memory loss is something that springs to mind, but if this is the case, you would need to be aware of how this might affect your presentation and be prepared to consider how you might address this in advance of attending court.

Culturally, some parents who are loving and solicitous of their child's wellbeing may not be used to thinking about their child's age in the way perhaps most parents might in the United Kingdom.

Again, if this is the case, it would be wise to address your mind to the different ways in which parents in your community or culture show interest or care in your children.

In connection with matters such as the age of your child, it pays to have an understanding of how children develop. Now, I am not suggesting that you need to become an expert on child development, but it would be advantageous for you to have some knowledge about factors such as the age children begin to crawl, walk, talk etc.

As well as being aware about matters such as your child's age, we live in a society where there is a cultural expectation to celebrate birthdays and festive seasons such as Christmas. So, if you do not buy your child Christmas or birthday presents, just be aware that your ex-partner may well choose to attempt to use this against you.

How you are perceived by the court is, or can be critical to your case, so it would be wise to think about how you might address such questions in the event you are asked questions related to this at court.

Whenever you can, it is to your advantage to highlight inconsistencies in your opponent's case and very helpful when you can provide evidence, which portrays a clear contrast between, for instance, your attempts to contact your ex-partner and his or her attempts to respond or reply to you.

Mr B was asked the following question: Well she would say that you didn't show any desire to be part of S's life. She has no record of you making contact with her. Do you see?

In response Mr B replied that he had contacted her on at least 6 occasions, that he clearly recalled between May and July and that out of those 6 occasions she had responded just once.

As stated earlier, if he had all the evidence of the dates he had called Ms C, his evidence would have been extremely convincing.

Expressing your evidence in this way, provides a very clear, graphic picture of Ms C's failure to respond to Mr B's phone calls. So if you get the opportunity to respond to a question in this way, it is always in your interest to do so, as the numerical differential evidence leaves little room for doubt, in the mind of those observing it.

Be aware when being cross-examined, that the lawyer does not always ask you a question. He or she may frame what you expect to be a question, but not actually ask it, leaving it hanging as a statement, or an unfinished question.

Under such circumstances, you must feel free to resist the temptation to comment or respond, unless you see an advantage to your case in doing so. Your self-control is often being tested by the lawyer, who wants to see what will spring forth from your lips that he or she can use to their advantage.

Sometimes the judge may intervene to ask that you wait for the lawyer to pose a question to you, before you respond.

Lawyers cross-examining you sometimes use this tactic because they are very much aware that parents giving evidence, or people in the witness box often feel, not only uncomfortable, being in the witness box, but additionally have difficulty managing periods of silence. Consequently, they may be inclined, in a knee-jerk reaction, to fill the vacuum left with words that have not been thought through.

In the statement below, the lawyer makes a statement which could be experienced as quite provocative to Mr B

"Ms C denies deliberately not answering your calls. Sounds to me like you're trying to shift the responsibility for your failure to recall the dates of the calls you say you made, onto Ms C."

As Mr B has not actually been asked a question, he could feel free to simply listen to the statement and not respond. There is no impetus to respond when being cross-examined when no question has in fact been posed.

Mr B then has an option to say nothing, wait for the lawyer to pose a question, or then failing to be asked one, decide how he wants to respond, if at all.

Mr B's response was a succinct and relevant one. "I am just trying to answer your questions as honestly as I can."

His response was brief and to the point, in that he had explained in his previous responses why he was thinking the way he was from the evidence he had gathered. Mr B had not chosen to rise to the bait delivered by the lawyer. He had remained calm and in control of his responses.

Answering or responding in this manner, presents an image to the judge of Mr B as being someone who is not swift to anger, as someone who respects the authority of the court, and possibly as someone whose evidence can be relied upon as being honest.

Of course, the judge would only come to this conclusion in the event that Mr B's evidence and presentation remained congruent throughout.

What I want you to contemplate is that, the whole time you are in the witness box, it is just a test – a 'stress test' of who you are and how you will perform when subjected to rigorous tests within a stressful, daunting environment.

So when the lawyer cross-examining you, asks you questions in a hostile or accusatory manner, what you need to do is not to consider the questions as a personal attack on you. Instead what you should do is to think about the questions and the entire process as an opportunity – your opportunity – to provide the court with your story, your account of what has been going on, that is consistent with the evidence and focuses on your child's best interests and wellbeing.

Whilst you are being asked questions by a lawyer and are doing your best to answer them honestly, you have to be alive to any questions which may pose a potential threat to your case or to how you may be perceived.

Sometimes lawyers will ask you a string of leading questions which seem very innocuous and straightforward, such that you do not have to think hard about how to answer them and can pretty much just agree with what you're being asked.

When this occurs you need to remain conscious that the more questions you answer in agreement with the lawyer, cross-examining you, the easier it becomes to continue to do so. This does not mean that you should disagree if you are sure you agree with what you are being asked. It is simply the case that you need to continue to have a healthy degree of wariness regarding questions posed to you.

Often lawyers will begin by asking you several questions that you will very likely agree with and then all of a sudden will slip in a question which takes you by surprise which you really have to think about before answering.

At other times lawyers will pose questions which you may instantly be aware pose a potential threat to how you are perceived.

For instance, when the lawyer began to ask Mr B questions about his height and weight and began to compare his size with that of Ms C, it should be instantly obvious what Ms C's lawyer was angling at. He was inferring that in some way – either consciously or unconsciously – that Mr B was being physically abusive to Ms C.

Getting Mr B to acknowledge the size difference between him and Ms C is a tactic which men in particular have to be aware of because it instantly produces an image in the mind of the judge of how slight or small Ms C is when compared to Mr B.

Fathers then have to be astute enough to recognise where the lawyer is leading the conversation towards. He then has to acknowledge that he is much larger than Ms C, and then go on to outline clearly why the court should believe that he at no time physically hurt or assaulted Ms C.

If Mr B failed to acknowledge that he is much larger and physically stronger than Ms C, it would indicate that he was either denying the obvious or lying. If Mr B failed to acknowledge this obvious fact, then it would add credence to Ms C's allegation that he physically abused her, because it would indicate that he has no awareness of the fact that he is physically much stronger than her.

People who are much bigger and physically stronger than you can harm you quite easily, without even meaning to do so. If you have ever had the unfortunate experience of accidentally being stepped on by someone twice your size and weight, you will readily grasp the point I am making.

The lawyer then goes on to put the argument to Mr B, that he not only physically hurt Ms C but traumatised S in the process, by arguing…

"So…when you got into a fight with her, from S's point of view, who was a quarter of her mother's size, can you see how traumatic that would have been for S to witness?

The lawyer's words then introduce the image or perception of a physical fight between the parents, with Mr B towering over Ms C and totally dwarfing S, who is naturally highly distressed at observing the incident.

The question gives rise to a number of matters, that Mr B has to address as follows:

"First of all I need to make this clear. I never fought with Ms C.,I defended myself, which means that when she was trying to hit and scratch me, I held her off as best I could. I did not hit her or shove her."

"Now, of course, I am much bigger than Ms C and we are both giants to S, and seeing this will have been very frightening for her, but at no time did she see me hit or physically harm her mother."

Mr B's response, then is to try to emphasise that although factually it was a fight or a brawl. It was not a situation in which he was actively engaged in fighting Ms C. Instead he was engaged simply at attempting to defend himself from her assault upon him without hitting, pushing or lashing out at her in any way.

He goes on to explain that of course he is physically bigger than both Ms C and S and acknowledges also that witnessing such an incident would have been very upsetting for S, whilst simultaneously stating that as adults, both he and Ms C were much bigger than S, but that at no time did S see him physically harm Ms C, as he never did so.

The lawyer cross-examining Mr B states further on that S is scared of him and that whatever closeness that used to exist between him and S, has changed now due to her observing traumatic incidents between them as opposed to any parental alienation from Ms C

Now Mr B's reply to the lawyer's argument is that he is prepared to see S at a contact centre, if that helps to alleviate Ms C's and S's alleged fears.

You might question why he should agree to comply with Ms C's proposal, since she has hardly gone out of her way to make it possible for him to see his daughter.

The reason is because if Ms C – the person with whom S lives with, is saying that S is frightened of her father, then in the absence of any other evidence, the judge is likely to feel forced to listen to what Ms C is saying. Not because he or she necessarily believes Ms C, but because if what the mother is saying is true, the judge recognises that unsupervised contact with Mr B, might harm S. So the best way forward under such circumstances, is for Mr B to gain contact with S via supervised contact.

This is a means towards getting his foot in the door and from there if he can prove that there is nothing wrong with his relationship with S under supervised conditions then he is on a much firmer footing to ask for greater contact at court at a later date.

If on the other hand he tried to dig his heels in and pressed the court to give him unsupervised contact, the likelihood is that the judge would either, order supervised contact and/or ask for a CAFCASS officer to see S and undertake a report on S's relationship with him and Ms C.

But that might mean that Ms C might be inclined to attempt to jeopardise the relationship with S further in the meantime, if unhappy with the outcome of the court hearing.

In addition, informing the court that you are willing to see your daughter even under supervised contact conditions indicates your commitment to the court and also means that during contact with S, an independent record of your time, and relationship with S will be documented.

What I am seeking to impress upon you, is the importance of avoiding getting into a competing or competitive mindset. The court is not so interested in who is to blame between parents. They are more impressed by a parent who can show that their behaviour and motivation is centred on safeguarding the welfare of their child.

Your job is not to get side-tracked or get your 'buttons pushed' which take you down a competitive, 'tit for tat' track. Your job is to remain alert, listen carefully to the questions, sift through the various answers you could give, and find answers which answer the questions truthfully, are congruent with what's in your child's best interests, and promotes you as being a balanced, caring parent.

Now let's turn to look at a Case Study involving a public law case

Case Study 3

Sarah Arthur a white British woman aged 34 has given birth to 4 children. Christine aged 16, Alison aged 14 and Tyrone Junior and Tia aged 6 and 3 respectively.

Christine and Alison are white, full siblings who were removed from Ms Arthur's care and adopted together 10 years ago.

Tyrone and Tia, both mixed race are half siblings, and currently in the care of their mother.

Ms Arthur had an unhappy and unfortunate childhood. She was the eldest child of her mother Ms Jean Arthur, who had two other children Elizabeth and Patrick Jackson aged 29 and 30 respectively.

Sarah Arthur never knew her father who disappeared from her life, so she was told, when she was about 2 years old. Her mother Jean was an alcoholic and had a number of male partners who both verbally and physically abused her.

Sarah Arthur was exposed during her childhood, not only to her mother's alcohol abuse and domestic abuse, she also suffered sexual abuse from one of her mother's male partners and chronic neglect whilst in the care of her mother.

Jean Arthur never showed Sarah love or had any time for her. It occurred to Sarah that her mother only had time, for the men in her life and invariably treated Elizabeth, and especially Patrick, much better than she treated her.

Sarah Arthur left school at the age of fifteen, she formed few friendships, frequently got into conflicts with others, and displayed difficulty concentrating in class. Her attendance was very poor and was in no way assisted by frequent changes of address.

Due to the poor care she received from her mother and her mother's male partners, she was placed in care for a couple of years when aged 14.

Two years after leaving care, she had a 3 year relationship with Christine and Alison's father – Tommy Green.

Mr Green was violent to her frequently, he both abused alcohol and drugs and the money from benefits, which should have been used to feed their children, was often spent on alcohol and drug use.

Ms Arthur's relationship with Mr Green ended after he was imprisoned for assault and armed robbery.

Ms Arthur then had a succession of male partners, who were abusive to her and one of whom sexually abused Christine.

The home environment that Christine and Alison lived in was unhygienic and chaotic.

The children were said to have moved homes ten times within a three year period.

Efforts were made to assist Ms Arthur in improving the care she offered her children but despite intensive support (which included Family Support Workers, Early Intervention workers, Health Visitors, social workers and a parenting course) Ms Arthur failed to make use of the support.

Consequently, Christine and Alison were made the subject of full care orders and subsequently adopted. Ms Arthur receives indirect letter-box contact twice yearly.

Ms Arthur suffered with depression for a two year period following her older children being adopted, then she met Mr Tyrone Ellis – a black British man, and had a three year relationship with him.

Their relationship was a stormy one, involving several allegations of physical violence perpetrated by Mr Ellis and numerous reports of verbal abuse which Tyrone Junior was exposed to. It was said by Mr Ellis and confirmed by Ms Arthur that she gave at least as good as she got.

Claire Roberts a social worker with whom Ms Arthur had developed a reasonably good trusting relationship with, had continually urged Ms Arthur to end her relationship with Mr Ellis, or run the real risk of history repeating itself by Tyrone Junior being removed and placed for adoption.

Eventually, Mr Ellis with the help of his family, made the decision to end his relationship with Ms Arthur. But they retained a form of friendship and Mr Ellis maintained for the most part, fortnightly contact with Tyrone Junior.

Some 3 months after Mr Ellis left Ms Arthur she commenced a new relationship with Brian White – a mixed-race man, the father of Tia. Mr White did not cohabitate with Ms Arthur, but stayed over a few times per week.

Concern about the care Tyrone Junior and Tia were receiving, heightened due to referrals from the nursery of Tia and the schools of Tyrone Junior. Although the relationship between the school, and nursery with Ms Arthur was described as mostly positive, the local authority received information stating that the children were attending sporadically, they presented at times as unkempt, tired and hungry.

Further concerns arose around the fact that the children had experienced three moves within a two-year period, which necessitated a change of school for Tyrone Junior.

Matters were made worse when the children were exposed to domestic abuse between Mr Ellis and Ms Arthur, Mr Ellis and Mr White and occasionally between Ms Arthur and Tia's father.

However, the situation as regards the children seemed to settle down when Ms Arthur's mother – Jean, who had been absent from her daughter's life for several years, came back into her life and seemed to have a calming influence over her daughter and the children's lives.

Sarah seemed more relaxed and the children presented better at school and nursery.

When Claire Roberts, who had been the allocated social worker for some four and a half years left, the children were subject to a Child in Need plan and plans were mooted about the children no longer needing to be subject to a plan.

The home environment was still poor, but it was felt by Claire Roberts that Ms Arthur was working cooperatively with the Family Support worker Tracie Smith.

Unfortunately, shortly after the social worker left, Tracie Smith left the department unexpectedly, and Ms Arthur was forced to work with both a new Social worker and a new family Support Worker.

Sonia Owusu – a social worker with 2 years of experience became the children's allocated worker in November 2018.

Ms Arthur was unhappy about the change of social worker and expressed her difficulty and unhappiness working with her to the team manager. She gave no other reasons other than saying she doesn't understand what the social worker was saying because of her accent.

The children's presentation worsened and their attendance at school and nursery declined in November and December of that year. Her relationship with her mother simultaneously markedly deteriorated following the introduction of a new man in her mother's life, resulting in a number of heated arguments and one incidence of violence, which was witnessed by Tia.

By December the children became subject to Child Protection plans under the category of Neglect, due to their continued poor attendance and unkempt presentation. But Ms Arthur often failed to allow the social worker access to the children and refused to cooperate also with the new Family Support Worker – Alina Smolenko.

Due to her failure to cooperate with professionals and Child Protection plans, the case was escalated to that of the Public Law Outline (PLO).

Following the PLO meeting, Ms Arthur was given two weeks to comply with the requirements of the meeting.

The requirements included the following:

Cleaning up and decluttering the family environment to a satisfactory standard.

Ensuring the children receive sufficient sleep and food consistently.

Ensuring the children attend school and nursery regularly.

The children are to attend looking clean, nourished and having had a sufficient amount of sleep.

Ms Arthur to cooperate with the social workers, keep appointments and allow the social worker and family support worker, access to the family home.

Ms Arthur was to ensure the children were not exposed to any further domestic abuse.

At the end of that same week Ms Arthur had a massive row with Brian White which was witnessed by both children and went into ‘melt down’ shutting off all communication with everyone. This resulted in the local authority initiating care proceedings on both Tyrone Junior and Tia.

Questions for Ms Arthur under cross-examination are as follows:

Q. Ms Arthur, you understand I ask you questions on behalf of the local authority?

A. Yes.

Q. You have…four children, is that correct?

A. Yes.

Q. Your first two of whom were adopted?

A. Yes.

Q. How old were you when you had your first two children?

A. 18 and 20.

Q. You…would you describe yourself as an experienced mother now?

A. …Well it don't come with a manual, but I guess I have some experience…it's relative I guess.

Q. Of course…But…you were the main carer for your first two children, yes?

A. Yes.

Q. And Tyrone Junior and Tia?

A. …Yes I am their main carer

Q. What roles, if any do their father's play?

A. Tyrone's dad has him for a weekend once per fortnight and occasionally he collects him from school.

Tia's dad shares her care with me when he's…when he stays with us…maybe two or three times a week.

Q. But you do the lion share of the care, for both, right?

A. Yes

Q. Now…I know it was several years ago, but what were the concerns the local authority had when your children were placed in care?

A. …There were concerns about the home not being tidy, or clean enough….there were concerns about the children's school attendance…and domestic fights and arguments.

Q. …And did you agree with any of these concerns?

A. …I agreed that there were fights between me and… one or two male partners.

Q. But, you didn't agree with anything else?

A. Not at the time, no.

Q. Not at the time! What about now?

A. I think the home could have been tidier…and that their attendance was not good.

Q. So…when you say it could have been tidier, are you now accepting that the local authority was right with regards to the lack of cleanliness within your home?

A. …I… I'm accepting it wasn't tidy enough –

Q. But, what are you saying as regards the standard of hygiene within the home?

A. I guess, it could've been cleaner, but it wasn't dirty.

Q. You don't sound too sure. Is it cleaner now?

A. Yes, I think so.

Q. OK. What about the children's school attendance, do you accept that the local authority was right to be as concerned as they were about your children's attendance?

A. I didn't at the time, but I guess they had their reasons.

Q. You guess they had their reasons! So, you don't fully accept, they were justified to be as concerned as they were?

A. Maybe..I'm not sure.

Q. You're not sure! It's been how long…10+ years?

A. Yes, about that.

Q. But you're still not sure. How much longer do you need, I mean if you had another 5 years do you think by then you'd know whether the local authority was right or not?

A. I don't know

Q. What about your children's presentation at school, do you recall whether the local authority had any concerns about that?

A. Yes, but I don't agree with them. My children went to school clean.

Q. I see, so the information from the school and the social workers at the time were incorrect, were they?

A ...People do make mistakes...and they can lie!

Q. Yes, but evidently not you! You would have the court believe that the social workers and school staff made mistakes and lie, whilst you were flawless, wouldn't you?

A. I'm not flawless, I just believe that in this respect they were wrong.

Q. Who lied?

A. The Family Support Worker and the social worker, my home was never dirty *

Q. Ok, that's what you want the court to believe is it?

A. Yes.

Q. Alright...So what would you say you learned from the experience of having your first two children placed in care and subsequently adopted?

A. Many things...I learned that life's not fair

Q. I mean specifically in terms of your parenting?

A. I learned that no one's perfect...that we all make mistakes and sometimes we need a second chance.

Q. I see…that's true we're all fallible, but I'm asking you about what you learned from the experience of losing your daughters?

A. I learnt that social workers say they want you to trust them, but they're just lying. They just want to take your children away.

Q. I see, so…what responsibility do you personally accept for your children being removed from your care?

A. …I think it wasn't a good time for me…The home could have been tidier, and the children didn't need to see the arguments and fights .. but no one's perfect and it was never dirty.

Q. Sounds to me like even now, many years later you still don't accept that the local authority were right to remove your children. Is that correct?

A. …I didn't at the time…I guess I still think if I'd had the support, things would have been different!

Q. What sort of support are you referring to? You had a social worker, a Family Support Worker and other -

A. I'm not talking about them, they were a waste of time. I'm talking about my mum, family, a partner I could rely on.

Q. Ms Arthur a moment ago you said life's not fair. Remember?

A. Yes.

Q. How fair has life been for your children?

A. …It hasn't been fair for them either!

Q. Yes but why? Who has made it unfair for your children?

A. Well the social workers didn't help!

Q. Ms Arthur, it's my understanding that you had a range of professional support at the time, was that not the case?

A. Yes, but they weren't helpful

Q. I see. Who was helpful?

A. …No one.

Q. What about you, does that include you?

A. …I was trying…but things were difficult.

Q. From your children's point of view, how helpful were you?

A. …Not…not helpful enough.

Q. So from your children's viewpoint, you couldn't make things fair for them either, could you?

A. …No, but for Tyrone and Tia, things are different.

Q. Are they?

A. Yes.

Q. What are the local authority concerns with respect to Tyrone Junior and Tia?

A. They say the children have been exposed to domestic abuse and their attendance at school and nursery is poor…but I don't agree that they looked dirty or tired.

Q. They say they've been exposed to domestic abuse, do you deny it?

A. I don't deny there have been arguments…I just think they exaggerate concerns sometimes.

Q. Can you remember any more of their concerns?

A. ...They say they present as hungry at school, but I don't believe that because at home they're always eating

Q. Ok. Anything else?

A. …Not that I can think of.

Q. What about the changes of accommodation and your unwillingness to allow professionals access to your home?

A. What do they expect me to do, if the landlord wants his property back

Q. I think the concern relates to the level of stability, you provide for your children. Do you see that?

A. If they were that concerned they'd have helped me to get my own secure tenancy by now.

Q. And what do you say about the concern that you're not allowing professionals access to your home?

A. I can't work with the social worker or the Family Support Worker.

Q. What's the difficulty you have with Ms Owusu – the social worker?

A. I can't understand her, she don't speak English properly and she don't listen.

Q. What about Ms Smolenko

A. Don't like her, she's too bossy and judgemental.

Q. Do you see any similarity between the current concerns and those that existed with your earlier children?

A. No, not really the circumstances are quite different. I'm in a better position now than I was then.

Q. You don't see any similarities with regard to the concerns the professionals had then and the ones they have now?

A. Well, in the past it was all about the tidiness and cleanliness of the home. That's not the issue now!

Q. Really, you don't think that's an issue! What do you see as the main issues now?

A. …They're on about things like, house moves and the children's attendance at school and nursery

Q. What about matters such as domestic abuse and fights with male partners.

A. It's different now…although we have had rows, for the most part I can rely on Tia's dad. I couldn't rely on anyone when I had Christine and Alison.

Q. I see…There have been a number of concerns about your care of your children, concerns which still exist more than ten years later. Perhaps you would be good enough, to explain to the court why your children, should remain in your care?

A. …Because I got support now from Tia's dad…. and because the children would be devastated…and because if I have to I will work with the social workers.

End of cross-examination of Ms Arthur.

As I hope will be quite obvious to you, I have chosen to make Ms Arthur answer in a way or manner which is unsuitable and very unlikely to produce a favourable outcome at court. I have done this because it is just as vital, to know what not to do (behave or say) as it is to know what to do and how to behave.

When the lawyer asks Ms Arthur whether she sees herself as an experienced mother, he wants to gauge her response so that he can use it to set her up, or use it to his advantage immediately or later.

If she says that she does not see herself as experienced, then he may be able to use this acknowledgement to argue that she was less experienced in the past and even now remains inexperienced and thus needing help with her parenting.

The fact that she was not appreciative or cooperative with the social worker and family support worker whilst accepting her inexperience, is not an attitude that I think presents her in the best possible light. Her answer exposes her to being perceived as ignorant and possibly arrogant.

Equally, on the other hand if she sees herself as an experienced parent and yet once again her actions or inaction have led to her children coming to the attention of the courts, it would likely force one to question her judgement and self-perception of her knowledge and ability.

Given these two possible answers, Ms Arthur's answer is suitable as it places her in between two extremes and allows a perception of her as being reasonably astute.

The lawyer then goes on to ask Ms Arthur whether she was the main carer for Tyrone Junior and Tia. The reason he or she would ask this question is because they want to establish that she is the main carer and thus responsible for the majority of care and the type of care her children receive.

One of the next questions the lawyer asks Ms Arthur is about her understanding of the concerns that existed when Christine and Alison were placed in care. Essentially, the concerns that existed during the care proceedings for Christine and Alison are very similar to the current concerns for Tyrone Junior and Tia.

The purpose of asking Ms Arthur this question is to examine Ms Arthur's understanding of the local authority concerns. If Ms Arthur does not understand, or has a very limited grasp of what the local authority concerns are, she is then in a less able position to address the concerns and satisfactorily meet the children's needs.

If she has a good understanding of the concerns but chooses to fail to co-operate with the concerns, unless she has a good reason for failing to co-operate, her actions suggest that she is wilfully neglecting her children.

The other purpose of asking Ms Arthur about the concerns of the local authority in the past was to test her awareness or insight concerning the similarity of the concerns. Her failure to recognise that the concerns were pretty much the same reveals to the court her lack of awareness, highlighting the point that Ms Arthur's parenting of her children has not changed in any significant way from the care she gave to Christine and Alison some ten or more years earlier.

Ms Arthur was asked whether she agreed with the concerns of the local authority when they removed Christine and Alison. Her response indicates a limited agreement at the time and even now, ten years later her answer gives a clear impression of only partial acknowledgement of the concerns, in that she only accepts concerns about domestic abuse, feels the home could have been tidier and the children's attendance could have been better.

Her response to these questions is unhelpful to her case because it demonstrates that the concerns she does not accept are areas where her children will likely continue to suffer harm and her failure to accept the concerns of the local authority some ten years later, provides a clear indication of her lack of understanding and insight.

Ms Arthur, like many parents, in my experience, is prepared to admit that her home could have been tidier but is unwilling to agree that her home was dirty.

Her reluctance to do so is understandable because no one wants to admit that their home is dirty or unhygienic. However, if the local authority has stated that one of the concerns about your parenting is that your home is dirty, they are very likely to have taken pictures or have other evidence which suggests that your home is, or at least was, unhygienic.

There are a number of ways in which the local authority can provide evidence which suggests there are sufficient concerns about the standard of hygiene within your home. These can include evidence from several professionals who have had access to your home. It could include professionals such as teachers or nursery staff who have observed the condition your child is in when he or she arrives at school or nursery.

Evidence gained from the police, neighbours, landlords, family members and your children can also be used against you at court.

So, it's really in your interests to do your utmost best to become more objective with regard to whatever claims are being made against you by the local authority or professionals.

Here I think it will be to your benefit to ask people who will be honest with you, whether they believe there is any truth in whatever concern the local authority has stated. It is important that you identify people who you can trust but who do not just think exactly the same as you do and are able to provide you with valuable feedback and advice.

Often at court parents are perceived as being 'wrong and strong.' In other words, everyone inside the court knows that your home environment is unsuitable for your children, even if not unhygienic.

It is clear by your actions that you (if like most parents in public law cases) will argue the point to the death to preserve your notion of pride. In the meantime, however, you fail to show the same strength of determination to ensure your children receive the quality and type of care that they need and deserve.

In the final analysis the question I would ask you to consider is: what's the most important consideration here, your pride or your children's wellbeing?

As Dale Carnegie argues in his book 'How to Win Friends and Influence People': "Any fool can try to defend his mistakes – and most fools do – but it raises one above the herd and gives one a feeling of nobility and exultation to admit one's mistakes." Carnegie goes on to argue: "When we are wrong – and that will be surprisingly often, if we are honest with ourselves – let's admit our mistakes quickly and with enthusiasm."

Why would admitting you are or were wrong be helpful to you, especially since it would likely be highly embarrassing to you?

The reason is, because it presents you as someone who displays decorum. The vast majority of people would never do this and this lifts you way above the average in the eyes of those observing you. For you to be so honest under these circumstances suggests that you are someone whose evidence can be trusted and relied upon.

It further exposes you as someone who is able to reflect and perhaps wrestle with your conscience which is something the majority of parents it seems tend not to do.

But if I do this won't it be used against me?

Well, the likelihood is that there is sufficient evidence to suggest that your home environment was, at the least, not suitable in the court's eyes so your denial is not really helpful.

Your honest acceptance, on the other hand, not only offers the benefits noted above, but also allows the judge to consider that you are someone who shows the potential to work with professionals to ensure that the concerns highlighted can be satisfactorily alleviated in the future and that is very much in your favour.

The cross-examiner goes on to ask Ms Arthur if her home is cleaner now than it was during the earlier proceedings. Her answer: 'yes, I think so,' doesn't exactly inspire one with confidence.

Just so that you as a parent are left in no doubt about what I am saying, if you want to leave the court with a positive view of your parenting currently, you would have to provide the judge with clear evidence that your parenting has changed and that despite what difficulties you had in the past, you are now committed to offering your children the best care you can.

You can't expect to go to court ten years after your earlier children were removed and present in a less than definite or clear manner concerning your thoughts and understanding of your past care of your children.

You have to present as having made definite changes, having recognised errors made in the past, unless you have new, substantial evidence which shows that you were unfairly treated during the earlier proceedings.

It is unwise to state as Ms Arthur did, that the professionals had made a mistake and/or lied about her children arriving at school unkempt or dirty. When care proceedings are instigated, your family law case will not have been presented before the attention of the court as a result of a whim, or without good grounds.

It costs the local authority money and its workers a great deal of time and effort to bring a case to court. The concerns that are then stated, such as your child arriving at school or nursery grubby or unkempt, are not events that have been noted once or twice. Instead they have been noted frequently despite discussions about the same and efforts made to improve matters over a period of time.

This does not mean that you as a parent have brought your child to school dirty every day. It simply means that it has been observed to have occurred with sufficient frequency to be noted and to be seen as habitual.

The chances then of professionals making a mistake or lying about this are unlikely. Just to be clear with you, I am not stating that professionals do not lie, but given that several professionals will likely have observed such events on a regular basis, the balance of probability is likely to weigh in favour of professionals.

In my view, it is always wiser to simply remark that to you, they appear to have made a mistake and go on to explain why you think it is a mistake. But you must have evidence to support your conclusion. If you do not have any real evidence to support your stance, then don't deny the concern.

As stated above, as long as you are being honest or genuine in your response, it is best to admit where or when you were wrong.

In addition, if you call a social worker, family support worker or a teacher a liar, then you need to be prepared to be taken through the evidence which supports their case in detail and in the process risk highly damaging yours.

When the lawyer asks Ms Arthur what she learned in terms of parenting, from or since the removal of her older children, that was Ms Arthur's chance to impress or dazzle the court with her parenting knowledge and skills.

It is her chance to demonstrate convincingly to the judge or the court that she has accepted responsibility for errors of the past and has developed the skills to provide her children with a good or much improved standard of care.

To say in response to the question: 'I learned that no one's perfect…that we all make mistakes and sometimes we need a second chance,' hardly provides the judge with the view that Ms Arthur's children will in the future, be spared the harm her children were exposed to in the past.

Her response does little to inspire confidence and under such circumstances, to talk in terms of needing a second chance when it seems apparent that lessons from the past have not been learned, would be tantamount to ensuring the children continued to receive the same poor level of care, since it is evident from her responses that she has failed to accept responsibility for the care she provided in the past.

Ms Arthur's answers to questions about the social worker and Family support worker expose her poor attitude towards professionals who are there to try to support her and improve her care of her children.

It never reflects well on you as a parent, to say negative or dismissive remarks about professionals. You do not have to like them or be friends with them but if you want to be perceived in a positive light at court you need to reflect a positive and cooperative attitude towards them.

Indeed, the likelihood is that if you maintain a relatively positive, co-operative attitude towards professionals in the first place, the chances of you needing to attend court and give evidence in a public law case are unlikely.

With regard to questions about domestic abuse, Ms Arthur does not deny there were arguments, but seeks to minimise the extent or impact of them on her children by saying that the social worker and family support worker exaggerated the concerns.

This would not be the attitude I would ever advise you take at court in connection with the Applicant's (local authority) concern related to domestic abuse.

Parents often fail to realise both the extent of the harm caused to children by seeing, hearing and being involved in domestic abuse and the frequency and extent to which children are aware of such abuse and conflict.

This being the case, it is never in your interests to try to minimise the concerns. You have to wake up to the potential harm to your children and show the court you take such matters seriously and have taken steps to ensure your children are protected from seeing or hearing domestic abuse.

Stating that professionals exaggerate such concerns as Ms Arthur did invariably guarantees that the judge cannot have confidence in your ability to safeguard your children.

When preparing to give evidence and when giving it, you should be very much aware of the concerns of the local authority. In my experience there is a tendency for parents in public law proceedings to miss out or overlook concerns, choosing or omitting to acknowledge the full extent of the concerns.

When asked whether she sees any similarities with regard to the concerns the professionals had in the past and the ones they have now, she replies: 'Well, in the past it was all about the tidiness and cleanliness of the home. That's not the issue now!'

So she assumes that the long term concern about the state of the home environment is no longer an issue, when it likely remains an issue, but just not as pressing as other concerns.

If you are hoping to present as a credible witness, you will have to consider and address your thoughts and answers to all the concerns of the Applicant. You can't try to brush their concerns under the carpet or ignore their existence because you don't consider them justified.

The last question posed to Ms Arthur about why the children should remain in her care or not be placed elsewhere is a fundamentally important one which you should have thought about and prepared a suitably convincing response to.

Your response needs to take into account all the concerns expressed and demonstrate your capacity to adequately meet them providing compelling reasons why it is not necessary and not in the children's best interests to be removed from your care.

The response you give should leave the court in no doubt that you are willing to work with the local authority and the professionals involved. In other words, you won't just work with professionals because you have to but instead, that you are committed to working with them in the best interests of your child/ren.

Of course, if in the past you have shown an unwillingness to work with the local authority and professionals, you will have to be very convincing in your explanation about why your attitude has changed now and how you can guarantee it will not revert back in the event your child remains in your care once the proceedings end

If you plan to present a comprehensive defence of your care of your child/ren you have to leave no stone unturned and be ready to address yourself to each and every concern.

Questions to the social Worker

As noted earlier during public law care proceedings, as a parent and as a social worker you can be cross-examined by a lawyer for each party. For the purposes of Case Study 3 Ms Owusu, as with Ms Arthur above, will be cross-examined as if there are only two parties involved in the case.

Q. Ms Owusu, you understand I will be asking you questions on behalf of Ms Arthur.

A. Yes

Q. Is it right that you became the allocated social worker in November 2018?

A. Yes.

Q. Prior to your involvement, Ms Arthur had developed a positive working relationship with Ms Roberts, is that your understanding?

A. Yes…as far as I know.

Q. She liked Ms Roberts didn't she?

A. Yes, I think so.

Q. She'd learned to trust her, hadn't she?

A. Again, yes I think so.

Q. When working with parents, do you agree it's very important to establish a trusting relationship with them?

A. Yes, when and where possible.

Q. I'm glad we can agree on that. Now, Ms Arthur had a very difficult childhood, didn't she?

A. Yes, from what I have read.

Q. She suffered neglect, rejection, abuse and less favourable treatment than her younger siblings, you're aware of that aren't you?

A. Yes I have read that.

Q. And she didn't just suffer one form of abuse, she was exposed to domestic abuse, alcohol abuse as well as sexual abuse. That's correct isn't it?

A. Yes, as far as I know.

Q. Likewise, she didn't just suffer one form of rejection. She suffered rejection from her father who she has never met and a mother who was an alcoholic and more interested in her male partners and her younger children. Didn't she?

A. Yes, I have read that.

Q. So, she had a troubled early family life and she also had a difficult time in school, didn't she?

A. Yes, certainly her secondary school education suggests that is the case.

Q. So can we agree that her life has been far from fortunate?

A. Yes.

Q. Good. Now let's have a look at the support that was offered to her. You've read the documents from the previous care proceedings, have you?

A. Yes, I have.

Q. Given her very unfortunate, neglected, abusive childhood, do you consider that she was provided with the appropriate level of support?

A. That's difficult for me to answer, as I was not the social worker at the time.

Q. I understand that, but you have read the previous bundles and you are aware of her background. Do you think she was provided with suitable support?

A. …I want to say that no one is infallible and it is often easier in hindsight to make judgements about what should and should not have been done.

I think Ms Arthur could have benefitted from therapeutic support to address sexual abuse and other abusive experiences. I gather that this may have been offered to her at, or around the time of the previous care proceedings, but do not think Ms Arthur availed herself of this opportunity.

I think, in addition, it was appropriate to offer Ms Arthur domestic abuse support. But again, I understand this was offered and not taken up by Ms Arthur.

Q. Ms Arthur disputes this, she says she has no recollection of being asked to consider these services.

A. My understanding, from the records was that she was offered these services, but chose not to avail herself of this support.

Q. Are you aware of any work that was undertaken with Ms Arthur following Ms Arthur's children being removed? I mean in between them being removed and before Ms Roberts became the allocated social worker?

A. I'm not aware of any work during that time.

Q. I see. Can you help me with this: do you know if Ms Arthur received any contact whatsoever from her children following their adoption?

A. I don't know…

Q. Well, who would know?

A. It's my understanding that the case was unallocated for a few years until it was allocated to Ms Roberts…the case would have been managed via the duty system I expect.

Q. So, the situation is like this, Ms Arthur's children have been removed and placed for adoption. She was meant to receive twice yearly letter-box contact with her children, but in fact receives no contact for almost two years. Were you aware of that?

A. No. I wasn't. I can only apologise to her for this. That must have been highly distressing.

Q. Well which manager or team should have been responsible to ensure contact occurred?

A. …The duty team I think. I will certainly make enquiries to discover what went wrong and who should have been responsible at the time.

Q. Thank you, I would be grateful… I wonder, were you aware that Ms Arthur suffered with depression for a two-year period after her children were removed?

A. I saw reference to this within the previous bundle.

Q. You see, it seems to me, that here we have a mother who's had an appalling childhood. Her children have been removed and adopted. No one bothers to check that she's receiving contact she's entitled to and understandably, she slips into a depression. It seems as though, once the children have been removed, the local authority have washed their hands of her. Do you think that's a fair summing up of what's gone on?

A. …I don't know why Ms Arthur did not receive indirect contact with her children, that's a serious error on our part that I am sorry she has suffered…I think as far as the local authority washing their hands of Ms Arthur, I can see how she might easily come to that conclusion.

The reality however is different, if the children are no longer deemed to be at risk of harm and Ms Arthur elects not to avail herself of the therapeutic support offered; then there's no further reason for professional involvement.

Normally, if there is a problem with contact or any other matter, Ms Arthur could approach duty, but it may be that her depression precluded her from doing so.

Q. Sounds to me that she received a poor service, wouldn't you agree?

A. As I said, I'm sorry about her not receiving contact, there's clearly been an error by the local authority in this respect. So, from that point of view, the service offered, at the time was not good enough.

In terms of her receiving professional support, she has to want to do this. We can't force Ms Arthur to remain involved with professionals if she does not want to be.

Q. It's understandable that she would not want to remain in contact with professionals who have removed her children, promised letter-box contact and then failed to deliver it.

A. It is the local authority's error…and it is unfortunate Ms Arthur did not feel able to bring it to the attention of the local authority at the time.

Q. Ok, let's move on. It is true that when Ms Roberts left the department that the children were on a Child in Need plan. Is that correct?

A. Yes it is.

Q. And the social worker's intention was for the children to come off the CIN plan?

A. …I am aware that the previous social worker thought this should happen at the time.

Q. I'm just wondering, did you have an opportunity to have a handover meeting with Ms Roberts before she left?

A. No, but I am clear about her position.

Q. How do you account for the different direction you took in this case?

A. …The plan that Ms Roberts intended to make occurred before Ms Arthur fell out with her mother, before the children's attendance and presentation worsened, before she exposed the children to further domestic abuse between her and Mr White and before she took the decision to refuse professionals access to her children.

Q. Yes, but you see, prior to your involvement, the social worker was talking about stepping the family down from CIN plans. Then immediately from your arrival, the case is stepped up to child protection, public law outline, to care proceedings. Someone's made another error haven't they?

A. Not from the evidence I have seen.

Q. You say no, but Ms Roberts knew Ms Arthur very well didn't she?

A. She worked with her for over four years, so I guess she felt she knew her quite well.

Q. Well…you say she felt she knew her, what do you mean by that? It seems to me she is likely to have known her far better than you!

A. …I mean that we can never really say we know people inside out…we may think we do and we may be right, but we could just as easily be wrong.

Q. It seems to me Ms Owusu, that it's much more likely that Ms Roberts knew Ms Arthur better than you, wouldn't you agree?

A. Clearly she knew her much longer than me…whether that meant that she knew all aspects of Ms Arthur's capacity to parent, is less clear.

Q. Ms Owusu, you have known Ms Arthur for what, four to five months at the most. Ms Roberts knew Ms Arthur some ten or twelve times longer than you. What makes you such an expert on Ms Arthur?

A. I'm not an expert on Ms Arthur, and I don't claim to be. But the evidence in this case indicates serious concerns about Ms Arthur's willingness to work cooperatively with professionals and with her ability to safeguard and protect her children.

Q. But with respect Ms Owusu, you have had the case for just...not even 5 months. And you've only got two years experience, that is correct isn't it?

A. Correct.

Q. But Ms Roberts had at least more than twice your experience. So what makes you right and Ms Roberts, who has much more experience and had known Ms Arthur far longer, wrong?

A. I am not standing here today saying Ms Roberts was wrong. She can only go on the information and evidence she is aware of. In the same way, that's what I have to do. I have to focus on the children, look at the evidence, and then come to decisions about how best to meet their needs.

Q. So, effectively what you're saying is, that we should disregard the fact that Ms Roberts knew Ms Arthur longer and has far more experience than you?

A. ...As I said, I can only go on the evidence that I am aware of at the time, and make informed decisions about how best to safeguard them and meet their current and future needs. And that's what I am doing.

Q. OK…You agreed with me earlier that when working with parents, it was very important to develop a good, trusting relationship, didn't you?

A. Yes, of course, when and where possible.

Q. Well Ms Roberts was able to do so wasn't she?

A. Yes it appears so.

Q. But you haven't, have you? What effect do you think your…less than positive relationship, has had on the outcome or position the family find themselves in?

A. …I can say that it probably hasn't helped at all, but I am mindful that the responsibility for fostering good relationships is not just my responsibility, it's Ms Arthur's also.

Q. You say it probably hasn't helped, but Ms Arthur went so far as to express her dissatisfaction of working with you to your team manager. Isn't that correct?

A. Yes, it is.

Q. So, the strength of her feeling or unhappiness about working with you is very likely to have had a detrimental impact on her state of mind, which we know will not have helped her care of the children. Do you follow my argument?

A. I understand your argument, but feel the need to assert a number of matters: it's her responsibility to make decisions and act in ways which keep her children safe and promote their healthy development; I am not responsible for the things that go on in her private life that may negatively impact on her care of her children, these things are not in my control and she also has to accept some responsibility for not just a poor relationship with me, but with Ms Smolenko also.

Q. Well Ms Arthur would say she gets on well with the professionals from the school and nursery. She's got no problems there, has she?

A. I think from what I have heard Ms Arthur, for the most part has been able to get on well with these professionals.

Q. So it's not the case that she has a problem with professionals generally is it?

A. The evidence doesn't suggest so, but despite this there remains clear evidence from these professionals which indicates serious concern about the care the children are receiving.

Another point which I think is relevant here, is that Teachers and Nursery staff are not the professionals whose duty it is to visit the family home and make difficult assessments about whether their children should remain in their care or not.

Q. Your argument doesn't hold water Ms Owusu because Ms Arthur had no problem working with both

Mr Roberts and Ms Smith, they were social work professionals who Ms Arthur had the pleasure of working with cooperatively for a number of years, that's true isn't it?

A. …Ms Arthur worked with them cooperatively for some years, however despite the support offered by professionals during the earlier proceedings, and that offered by the professionals you have named, Ms Arthur's recent behaviour has demonstrated serious concerns, about her ability to keep her children safe.

Q. There's been a lot of talk about the current concerns mirroring the concerns that existed with Christine and Alison, for example the number of moves the children have experienced. Where do you stand in this regard?

A. With regard to the number of moves Tyrone Junior and Tia have had, three moves is small when compared to the ten moves Christine and Alison experienced. But I am aware that Ms Arthur has had difficulty obtaining suitable accommodation for reasons that aren't always within her control.

Q. I am happy to hear you have taken a conciliatory approach, but what are your views about the ten moves the older children of Ms Arthur experienced?

A. …What we know is that moves are disruptive and stressful for all of us and this is likely to be very destabilising for children's education, health and development. But I wasn't working with the family at the time, as you know and don't know the circumstances which led up to these reported moves.

Q. Well I've done some research into these moves. What would you say if I was to tell you that seven of those ten moves were not as a result of the actions of Ms Arthur at all? What if I was to tell you they were the direct result of the actions or inaction of the local authority?

A. …I would listen to you carefully and be interested to understand how this happened.

Q. I hope so because seven of those moves occurred when the children were accommodated. Now I am not suggesting for one moment that the local authority meant to do this, but the way the information in the documents is written, one could be forgiven for assuming that these moves were down to Ms Arthur. It's not fair is it?

A. If what you say is the case, it certainly isn't, and it needs to be corrected and adequately addressed, but the current concerns remain highly relevant.

Q. Yes, but my point Ms Owusu, is that the local authority is quick to focus on the harm caused by Ms Arthur but silent about the serious harm they themselves have caused. What do you say about that?

A. …I think if and where the local authority has caused harm or instability to the children, then you're quite right to highlight it as a serious issue that needs to be looked at, just as the current concerns identified regarding Tia and Tyrone Junior need to be.

Q. I am grateful for your views. Now, the local authority has been concerned about Ms Arthur's choice of partners. Is this a matter that you are worried about?

A.…It's certainly been a concern in the past. Domestic abuse has been an issue and it remains an issue currently, although I have very recently spoken to both Mr White and Mr Ellis and those conversations have been for the most part positive.

Q. I'm glad you have spoken to the fathers because it seems that concerns have unfairly focused on the mother, whilst the problems they have caused have been overlooked. Their role in these disturbances needs to be properly assessed, don't you think?

A. It will be important to look at both the fathers' and Ms Arthur's role in the incidents concerned, but doing so and ensuring the children are well and safeguarded is very difficult to do if Ms Arthur chooses to refuse professionals access to herself and her children.

Q. I have spoken to Ms Arthur and of course, she recognises the importance of working with professionals…it's just that she's used to working with professionals she has no difficulty understanding.

You do understand that your accent is quite strong unfortunately and that Ms Arthur at times struggles to understand what you're saying to her?

A. I understand this fully…I sometimes struggle to understand what she is saying to me. It is for this reason that I put important information in writing to her (I've asked Ms Smolenko to do the same) and try to listen attentively to whatever she says to me. It takes up more time, but if it helps us to understand each other better, then of course it's worth doing.

Q. …Well, yes except Ms Arthur's reading is not that good, she thinks she's Dyslexic. Did you know that?

A. No. I had an inkling her reading wasn't very good, but she has not been that willing to have conversations with me and consequently I admit that I have not had much opportunity to ask her about her ability in this area.

Q. Now that you know she is Dyslexic, what help will you make available for her?

A. I am open to looking at any ways in which we can help improve our communication. I will explore any services that may assist. I am aware from my discussions with Mr White that Ms Arthur sometimes asks him to read communication from us, so as to ensure she understands it. Ultimately however, I hope she will feel able to give her input into this.

Q. You've spoken to Tyrone Junior and Tia haven't you?

A. When I have been able to.

Q. You've discussed with them their wishes and feelings?

A. Yes, I have.

Q. When did you last see them?

A. I saw them 8 days ago, at school and at Tia's nursery

Q. And what did they tell you?

A. They told me they both want to continue living with their mother.

Q. Did you enquire how they would feel if they were forced to live with someone else?

A. Yes I did

Q. What did they say?

A. Tia couldn't answer. Tyrone Junior said he would feel very sad.

Q. Help me with this please. If the children were placed elsewhere, what harm would they likely suffer?

A. If the children were placed elsewhere, as they are attached to their mother, they would of course miss her a great deal, this would likely be traumatic for them.

Depending on where and with whom they were placed, the children might have to change school or nursery and get used to other changes, such as seeing their mother and family members at arranged contact dates and times.

But the harm they would suffer has to be balanced against the harm they have been suffering over most of their short lives to date and in the absence of Ms Arthur being willing to cooperate, avail herself of support offered and make changes, it is clear these children will continue to suffer significant harm.

Q. What harm do you say the children have suffered?

A. The evidence suggests that they have suffered neglect in the form an unhygienic home environment, a lack of appropriate routines, which has meant that the children do not get sufficient sleep, are not consistently fed and provided with the appropriate physical care it is reasonable to expect they should receive.

In addition, the children have been subjected to domestic abuse between not only Ms Arthur and the fathers of the children, but also Ms Arthur and her mother.

Q. A few moments ago you said that Ms Arthur wasn't willing to work with you and make changes, but that hasn't really been tested has it?

A. ...Well that's where I would disagree with you. It was tested during the previous proceedings and it has been tested within the last four months that I have been working with her.

Q. Yes, but that was before you knew of her dyslexia. Surely the children deserve a chance to be brought up by their mother and not have to endure the harm you mentioned earlier?

A. The children deserve and require a standard of care that consistently meets their current and long term needs. I accept that we did not know that Ms Arthur was dyslexic, but we have really been trying to support her as much as we can, but I have to say, she has not helped herself and in the process has continued to offer her children a poor standard of care.

The fact that she has difficulty reading and writing does not, in my view, justify her unwillingness to work with Ms Smolenko and myself. I think we have the same difficulty understanding her, but it's about being willing to take the time to try and adopt a co-operative attitude.

Whether she likes me or not, is not important, it's about putting her children's needs first, which is something she has continued to demonstrate an inability to do with the outcome that they continue to suffer harm.

Whilst I recognise that she has experienced many difficulties, my focus has to be on the children and on what, from the evidence, would appear to be in their current and long term best interests. In my submission, there is no evidence to suggest that Ms Arthur at this time can meet the children's needs.

End of questions to Ms Owusu.

The lawyer begins the cross-examination of Ms Owusu by asking several questions designed to obtain a 'yes' answer to. They do so often because they know from experience or training that the more frequently you answer 'yes' to their questions, the easier it is to continue to do so.

A tactic lawyers use is to begin their cross-examination of you with tepid questions that are easy to answer, in that they don't require you to think much when answering them or give rise to any conflict between you and the lawyer.

However, they craft questions which turn up the heat or pressure on you as a witness slowly, such that you may not recognise the gradual building up of pressure and may then not be prepared to answer the harder or more critical questions.

The questions about Ms Arthur's relationship with the previous social worker, Ms Roberts, are all leading up to being critical or blaming of Ms Owusu in some way.

Social workers when answering these questions are right to agree with the lawyer whenever it is obvious that what the lawyer is saying is correct. However, you need to be very much aware of where the lawyer is going or attempting to lead you.

When the lawyer asks Ms Owusu whether she agrees when working with parents that it is very important to establish a trusting relationship with them, again the obvious answer is yes, but Ms Owusu adds a caveat, she states 'when and where possible.' In doing so, she paves the way to argue or explain later that trusting relationships can only be established by the individuals concerned – they are not the responsibility of one person only.

The lawyer then goes on paint the true and painful childhood history of Ms Arthur. Again the lawyer is working up to getting an agreement from the social worker about how awful Ms Arthur's childhood and life has been.

Then the lawyer then slips in a question about whether Ms Owusu has read the documents from the previous proceedings?

Ms Owusu agrees that she has done so. If she had not, the lawyer would have used this opportunity to criticise her or undermine her credibility as a witness.

The lawyer, armed with this information, introduces the question about whether the social worker thinks the services and support offered to Ms Arthur was appropriate, given the nature and extent of her troubled and abusive past.

Ms Owusu initially responds that it is difficult for her to answer as she was not involved at the time.

The lawyer, well aware that it is a 'tricky' question, persists to pressure her for a response.

The social worker answers this question quite skilfully, again making room for, or paving the way for a credible answer that the lawyer may not want her to make. By explaining that no one is infallible and that it is often easy to be critical of others with the benefit of hindsight, both of which are truthful and sensible points, she makes any possible errors of judgement appear more understandable when looked at in that light.

She then explains from her understanding of the local authority records what was offered to Ms Arthur.

The lawyer may then have been shocked by her answers because she was offered largely appropriate support, but had no memory of being offered such support, which may account for the reason Ms Arthur did not take up the offer of support available to her.

The lawyer moves on to question, the social worker about whether she was aware, that Ms Arthur did not receive indirect contact with her children for a period of time, following their adoption.

Ms Owusu's reply is an apologetic response, although she was not the social worker responsible for this error, she makes it clear that she is very sorry that the error occurred.

She doesn't act dismissively and say she wasn't involved at that time, or that it has nothing to do with her. She behaves in a compassionate, empathic manner, consistent with a professional who seeks to foster a trusting, cooperative working relationship, and to be perceived as a credible professional witness.

When Ms Owusu is asked her view of whether she thinks Ms Arthur has received a poor service overall, she responds by saying with regards to Ms Arthur not receiving the indirect contact she should have received, that the service she received at that time was poor, or not good enough.

The social worker then makes it plain which part of the service which was not good enough at the time and goes on to articulate, that the local authority can only offer professional support and it is up to Ms Arthur to accept, or reject the support offered.

The cross-examiner then begins to ask questions leading up to the obvious difference of opinion between Ms Roberts' view at the time she left the department and Ms Owusu's current assessment of what was in the best interests of the children.

Here, the social worker will need to be aware that she has already answered questions by the lawyer that highlight that Ms Roberts is a much more experienced social worker and had the advantage of working with Ms Arthur far longer than Ms Owusu.

Ms Owusu then, quite rightly, points to the importance of her intervention and view being guided or based upon the recent concerning information.

In essence then, Ms Owusu is saying that, however experienced a social worker is, and no matter how long one has known and worked with a parent, that professionals focused on the safety and wellbeing of children must look at the presenting concerns and (keeping the children's needs at the forefront of their mind) come to informed decisions about how best to proceed.

She also, appropriately, points out in the manner in which she answers questions that working with someone and having the benefit of being involved with them for a long period of time, does not necessarily mean that you know them well, or that you know all aspects of that person's character and behaviour.

The lawyer attempts to shift the reason and responsibility for Ms Arthur's actions, onto the poor relationship between the mother and the social worker, but Ms Owusu makes it clear where Ms Arthur's responsibilities, as the mother of her children should lie.

The cross-examiner continues on to suggest that Ms Arthur was able to work perfectly well with a number of other professionals, thus inferring that Ms Owusu herself was the problem in this case.

The social worker explains that although the lawyer is focusing on the current poor relationship between Ms Arthur and herself, that what is significant in terms of Ms Arthur's capacity to meet her children's needs, is that she received the support of Ms Roberts for over four years and the support offered during the previous proceedings. Despite receiving this support from professionals she trusted (clearly this was so, with regard to Ms Roberts and Ms Smith) the current evidence does not demonstrate that she has been able to satisfactorily meet her children's needs for safety and stability.

Ms Owusu was asked about the sheer number of moves Alison and Christine had, which were, the lawyer said, incorrectly attributed to the care given by Ms Arthur.

This, if correct, is dangerous misinformation spread by the local authority. It is thus vital to question and query information you receive since it may not always be correct.

The social worker, in my view, acts correctly by expressing her appropriate concern regarding the dissemination of such false information and stating that enquiries need to be made to see how this occurred, in order to prevent this ever happening again.

Nevertheless, she also makes it clear, that she is not going to be derailed by this information and that the current concerns are significant and need to be focused on.

The lawyer attempts to refocus the social worker's thoughts on the behaviour of the fathers, in this case suggesting that Ms Arthur has been unfairly blamed and targeted for criticism.

Ms Owusu, like all competent social workers, has to keep her eye on the ball and maintain a full (as opposed to partial) picture of who, and what needs to be investigated.

She also articulates that she has as much difficulty understanding Ms Arthur as Ms Arthur says she has understanding her and basically, that she is doing all in her power to facilitate better communication between the two of them. She leaves unsaid the quite obvious fact that she can only go so far and that Ms Arthur has to try to meet her halfway.

Ms Owusu also chooses not to mention that she suspects that part of the reason Ms Arthur does not like her or Ms Smolenko, is because Ms Owusu is a black African and Ms Smolenko is eastern European.

She wisely, in my view, is silent in this regard because she does not feel she has clear enough evidence to support her suspicions, or that it would necessarily help her case in bringing the matter to the attention of the court.

It is necessary to bear in mind that, as a social worker you can never assume that parents can read and write.

Indeed, it is key to be cognizant, that parents may often seek to hide or disguise their inability in this area.

In the event that a parent has difficulty reading and writing, your role is to try to take this into account and to facilitate their understanding as much as possible, so that you can make an informed assessment of their capacity to care for their children.

Always be prepared, in the event that your care plan is one of removal of the children, to be asked a question about what harm the children will likely be exposed to as a result. In coming to a decision that it's in the children's best interests to be placed elsewhere, you have to factor into your argument, the real distress and harm the children will experience due to the change of placement.

Of course the benefits of removal have to outweigh leaving the children in their mother's care, even when taking into account any supports that could be provided.

In the event that you assess that the children need to be removed, you will have to be prepared to explain in detail why this draconian action is necessary. You will also have to answer the question of whether any resources and supports could be implemented now, to safeguard and secure the children's wellbeing at home, within the children's timescales.

This question requires you to consider whether there is any support/s that could be provided to Ms Arthur, which would likely enable her to be able to offer her children suitable, or 'good enough' care within a period of time, such as six months.

The children's timescale is invariably a short period of time, because the reality is that children need appropriate consistent care now, or failing that, they require it as soon as possible, in order to avoid suffering further harm that would likely jeopardise their emotional health and wellbeing.

As your role as a social worker is about meeting children's, needs now and throughout their childhood, they cannot wait for parents, who are unfortunately not able to care for them adequately, currently, or within the foreseeable future.

This sets you up to receive much censure, because the nature of the job (as you know) is one which readily attracts criticism from all parts of society and despite your hard work and best intentions, very rarely do you receive the praise you deserve.

Lawyers, I consider, generally perceive social workers as easy targets – defenceless prey, ready to be ripped to pieces in the witness box, by legal wolves. You may think I am being overly dramatic, and that lawyers are just doing their job. Well, that is true they are, but so are you…and it is a difficult, demanding, demoralising and often a thankless job. So why should you allow your hard work to be ridiculed, devalued and rubbished?

One day – and this may be just a dream that never comes to fruition – I hope society wakes up and begins to value social workers with the appropriate level of reverence you deserve. But human nature is such that people do not tend to respect you until you defend, and respect yourself. Giving credible evidence at court, displaying a suitable level of pride, professionalism, dignity, poise and empathy is your best way of demonstrating your self-respect.

Key Learning Points

- Answer the questions asked of you.
- Where possible, back-up your evidence with examples and exhibits which prove or support your claims.
- Try to be measured and balanced in your responses.
- Use statistical evidence whenever possible to prove your point/s.
- Remember that there are often a number of ways to answer a question put to you. Choose the way that best conveys your argument and focuses on the needs of your child.

- Show in your answers that you are empathic towards your child and are able to prioritise his or her needs.
- Do not be tempted into competitive behaviour. Remain solely focused on your child's welfare.
- Accept responsibility for your actions and any mistakes. Do not be afraid of admitting when you are wrong. There is nothing to be gained from adopting a 'wrong and strong' attitude.
- It's important to know your child's age and to send them birthday cards and presents on their birthday and at Christmas, unless you have a different faith.
- Try to be aware of where the lawyer is leading you with their questions.
- If you have experienced certain circumstances before and history is repeating itself, you will demonstrate to the court, poor insight if you are unable to recognise that your current circumstances mirror an earlier one.
- If you have not accepted the concerns of professionals in the past and continue to show denial or limited acceptance of past concerns, you demonstrate to the court your lack of willingness to change.

- Keep your mind focused on the macro or bigger picture. Be prepared to accept, for example, that your home was dirty. It is better to lose the battle and give yourself the best chance of winning the war.
- Be careful to avoid making assertions about the other parent or professionals unless you have clear evidence that supports your claims.
- Be aware of the attitude you are showing others and demonstrate your willingness to work co-operatively with professionals. You do not have to like them.
- Never attempt to minimise the harm caused to your child from witnessing domestic abuse. Be aware of the harm caused by exposure to it.
- Be fully prepared to argue why it is in your child's best interests to remain in your care.
- As a social worker, be clear where your responsibility begins and ends. But remember also you are part of the local authority and are thus unable to divorce yourself fully from their actions.
- Do not allow your professionalism as a social worker to be undermined by comparisons between you and other social workers and

professionals. Stick to your understanding of the concerns posed to the child from the totality of the evidence before you.

- Where necessary, be prepared to check the source and reliability of the information given to you about children and parents. It is not always correct.
- Recognise that parents often seek to hide the fact that they have difficulty with literacy, and work to facilitate appropriate communication between yourself and the parent.
- Be prepared to accept questions about the harm that would be caused to a child by being removed from their parent or caregiver, and balance this with the harm they would likely suffer, if they remained at home.
- Consider the support or intervention that could be implemented, to alleviate the harm to the child so as to preclude the need for their removal.

Now, let's turn to look at some of the mistakes you can make, as well as the things you must do, whether as a parent or social worker when appearing at court to give evidence.

The 'Do's And Dont's' Of Giving Evidence

"***You have to learn the rules of the game, and then you have to play better than anyone else.***"

Albert Einstein.

There are lots of things you may have to do in life, which you may find stressful. Driving a car for example, can be very stressful, particularly when you first start having lessons, when you can't control your vehicle and do not know the rules of the road. Once you master control of your vehicle and know the Highway code, driving becomes a familiar experience and then easy, because you do the same things over and over again.

Giving evidence at court is no different, it is simply that you are highly unlikely to give evidence frequently enough for you to become as accustomed to doing so, as driving your car.

It is because I have given evidence probably, one hundred or more times that I have no doubt that the guidance and principles I offer you below will help you navigate the rigours of cross-examination successfully – providing that is, that you follow them.

Before going to court, make sure you dress appropriately. **Wear formal attire.** I would not advise you to wear a pair of jeans, a 'hoodie' and trainers. If you are a woman, dress as you might for a job interview. **Do not wear revealing outfits**.

This may seem ridiculous to you, but we all judge people on sight, before we interact with them in any way. You have done it, I have done it, and although the judges may be learned and wise, they do it also – it's human nature.

Now, of course judges use a range of other factors, to assess you, but why not give yourself the best opportunity, to be seen in a positive light? Remember, he or she does not know you. You have just one shot to make a good impression. To do so, every part of you needs to be congruent.

You're attending a court of law, which is about to decide something very important, to you and your child/ren. So the best thing to do is, treat the court respectfully by dressing suitably.

When going into the courtroom, make sure you **turn your phone off.** You do not need distractions when giving evidence.

It is a good idea to go to the toilet shortly before going in to court. Of course you will not always know when you will be called in, but if you need a break to attend the toilet, or to clear your head, **you may ask the judge for a short break**.There is no harm in you doing so. But **do so only when there is a break in your questioning**.

Do not do so in the middle of answering a question. Answer the question first and then request a short break.

When asked to sit down in the witness box, **sit back and make yourself as physically comfortable as you can.** Take deep breaths to relax yourself; the water and cups on the desk are placed there for you, should you require them.

During your examination-in-chief and cross-examination, **avoid any inclination to criticise others.** You do not need to berate anyone, simply explain any differences between you and the person, or persons you are talking about and give your reasoning and evidence to support your case.

In my view and in my experience, you rarely, if ever, gain points from being critical of others. That is what the majority of parents do. If you want to stand out from the crowd, do something different. Instead of criticising, where you can, **praise others.**

Demonstrate to the judge that you have the ability to be balanced and fair, that you recognise any positive things that your ex-partner or opponents have done.

This will likely impress the judge far more than you being critical. Criticism only gives rise to resentment, and attracts the same back towards you. Just imagine for a moment how much more peaceful your child's world (and everyone else's) would be if we were inclined to genuinely praise much more, and criticise far less.

You may be asked many questions when in the witness box. If you do not know the answer to the question, **do not guess or speculate,** just answer by stating that you do not know the answer. In the event that it is a question you consider you should know the answer to, then take the time to think through the circumstances, context, or reasons why you cannot answer that question.

Sometimes as a parent or as a social worker, you may be asked questions which are beyond your knowledge, or sphere of expertise. Always take the time to think about whether you are in a position, to answer the question or not**. Do not answer questions about matters where your presence was essential in order to answer it, if you were not present,** other than to comment that you cannot answer it because you were not there at the time.

In addition, as a social worker **do not answer questions which are beyond your remit.** Simply explain, for instance, that you are not a psychologist or doctor and thus do not feel able to comment on matters outside of your area of knowledge.

It is a lawyer's job to ask you questions, which at times put you on the spot, get under your skin and annoy you. Accept this as a reality. **Do not be tempted to argue with lawyers or the judge. Be courteous at all times.**

Do not answer questions in a defensive manner; your goal is to be seen as a credible witness. You cannot be perceived as credible, if you present defensively, or in a guarded manner.

Do not ask questions of the lawyer cross-examining you. This is not your role, your role is to listen intently to the question, to remain calm and when ready to do so, answer the questions asked of you.

Do answer questions in an open, thoughtful, constructive manner.

When answering questions, **wait until the lawyer has finished speaking before attempting to answer the question.** It is perfectly acceptable to ask the lawyer, to repeat the question if you did not hear it properly or did not understand it.

Do ask the lawyer to repeat the question or to rephrase it if it does not make sense to you, or is unclear. This is a tactic you can use to allow you more time to be clear on what you are being asked, and to think about how you intend to answer it.

When answering questions, **look at and give your attention to the judge,** as it is he or she, who most needs to hear your evidence. My advice is to angle your head in the general direction of the judge and fix a spot that you feel comfortable gazing at whilst listening to questions put to you. Then look at the judge when answering.

This prevents you from having to keep moving your head from the lawyer to the judge. It is not a sign of rudeness, it is appropriate that you focus on the judge when responding to questions. If you follow this advice, you are less likely to be distracted by the person cross-examining you.

Be prepared to be led by the judge at all times. If there is an objection by a lawyer or the judge interrupts, **follow whatever direction the judge gives and be guided by what they ask you to do.**

Answer the question asked but **do not be inclined to volunteer information,** unless the information you give explains the situation better, and you are sure it is helpful to your case.

Ask the judge if you can use your notes to refresh your memory, if you are asked to confirm a specific date that you can confirm from consulting with your diary, or explain events of an incident, that you wrote about at the time. Advise the judge that you made a note of whatever you are being asked, in your diary or notebook, and request whether it is okay for you to refer to your notes or diary.

Listen carefully to the question, remain focused and do not get side-tracked or be tempted to waffle.

Like driving a car when you are inexperienced, **do not rush.** Take your time and think through your answers. Just like discourteous drivers, the lawyer may attempt to rush you, but you need to **remain in control of your thoughts and emotions** and answer when you are ready. There is no reason to rush. The person who needs to hear your answers is the judge, and under normal circumstances, they cannot write as fast as you speak, so take your time and speak slowly and clearly.

Do not be afraid of silence when giving your evidence. The judge knows that what you are being asked to do is not easy. So do not put yourself under more pressure than you need to be under, by rushing to answer questions. That way you are pretty much guaranteed to make mistakes.

Do not be frightened of the judge. This of course, is probably easier said than done, for most people. Nevertheless, you gain nothing by being too fearful of the judge. Your aim is to be balanced, respecting the judge and being led by them whenever they instruct, you to do something; but remaining willing and able, to put over your belief and point of view, preferably ones which are supported by the evidence. Being too timid never impresses anyone.

If you make a mistake, admit it and correct it as soon as you become aware of it. There is no harm in explaining to the judge that you made a mistake in your answer to a question, although obviously if this happens more than once or twice at the most, it does begin to undermine your credibility.

When giving your evidence **do not lie**.

You have given your oath or affirmation, so one of the most serious and detrimental mistakes you can make whilst giving evidence at court, is to lie.

It is suspected that many parents do so, but it is one of the worst things you can do for the following reasons:

Firstly, if you lie, you are taking a huge risk, as your lie/s may be exposed during cross-examination, which will inevitably be harmful to your case, because you will have shown yourself to be someone whose statements and evidence cannot be trusted.

As a consequence, how can you expect the court to believe anything you have said? If you are willing to lie following making an oath or affirmation, it provides a clear negative statement about your character.

Secondly, even if you get away with it at court, it is something that is on the record and lies have a pernicious habit of coming back to 'bite' you at a later date, with disastrous consequences.

You may notice that the wording on the oath and affirmation is very precise, regarding the expectation, concerning the evidence you give. There is not just a requirement that you tell the truth, there is a requirement that you tell the entire truth as far your knowledge and understanding permits, and that you confine your evidence to the truth alone.

This brings me onto another point, which is important for me to share with you. When you are giving evidence, for example, about your relationship with your ex-partner, you may be asked questions which, you may consider will show you up in a 'bad' light.

Let's use the example of you being asked whether it is true that your ex-partner tried to contact you on numerous occasions, without success, for the purpose of arranging a time when he could have contact with his child?

Let us also assume on this occasion, that this is a true account of what has gone on.

On first sight, this information would appear to be evidence that shows you up in a negative light. As a result, fearing the assumed response from the court, you might be inclined to lie, or fabricate your evidence in some way, to make your behaviour appear more reasonable.

However, if you concede that this did in fact take place, as suggested by answering 'yes,' you may then go on to either state that in hindsight, you are sorry for behaving in this way. If indeed you are.

Do not be afraid to say sorry when you are wrong. Be willing to acknowledge when and where you are wrong, or where you have made mistakes. **Be willing to accept responsibility** or at least your share of responsibility for things that have gone wrong.

Bear in mind that the judge does not expect you to be a paragon of virtue. But if you assume responsibility, and are genuinely sorry, it does your case no harm at all. At least the judge can see, from your character that you have the ability to show remorse and take responsibility for problems.

Many parents never genuinely show any sign of this at court and their failure and shortcomings in these areas, does not go unnoticed. In my view, it often harms their case.

Just remember that one of the reasons giving evidence at court is so daunting, is because you, your character, attitudes and behaviour are under the microscope. You are being observed, examined and evaluated. So, think about that and be conscious of it when you make decisions. Also, **be aware of your body language when giving evidence.** To give credible evidence, what you say has to be congruent with the way you say it.

If you have ever observed someone talking about something that they are not confident about, you will know what I mean, their body language betrays them.

My advice is to practise giving evidence in front of a mirror or in the presence of a friend.

Now, getting back to the example of you choosing not to respond to your ex-partner's attempts to contact you, there might be a number of reasons, for you doing so. The problem for some parents is that, you may be so worried and distracted by how it might come across in court, that you fail to go on and answer the question fully.

In other words, you have told the truth, but not the whole truth. Due to your anxiety and perhaps, lack of understanding, you might fail to realise that you have more to add to that answer.

You have to be aware that this is your opportunity to explain fully what has been going on. The person cross-examining you will only want you to answer their questions, in a way that suits their client's case. You have to **be willing to explain yourself fully.**

After you have answered 'yes,' they may then wish to silence you by asking another question, or by saying something cutting, designed to rattle you.

Your job however, is to expect this whilst being cross-examined, and go on to explain why you felt it necessary not to respond to your ex-partner, in the way you did. Be prepared to **be assertive** under these circumstances and note that I am advising you to be assertive, **not aggressive or rude**.

You might for instance, need to speak up and say words to the effect of: "I am sorry, I had not finished giving you my answer…The reason I did not respond to your client when he made contact with me is because…"

It may be that you were justified in not responding to him, but if you don't explain the reasons fully, then the judge can only consider the information or evidence placed before them. On explaining the circumstances fully, the judge then has been provided with the evidence with which to come to a decision, concerning whether you were justified, unreasonable, or whether there were extenuating circumstances for what appeared to be unreasonable behaviour.

What might the judge consider as extenuating circumstances, you might ask?

Well it could be, that you decided not to return his calls because you knew from past experience that although he was contacting you saying that he wanted a discussion about the children, that instead he habitually displayed controlling and abusive behaviour towards you, such as bombarding you with text messages and phone calls whilst demonstrating no interest in the children.

Under such circumstances, it would be helpful for you to provide dates in which this bombardment took place, because if you can show that during the course of a week, for example, he contacted you 50 times, and that this is, or was a familiar pattern in the way he behaved towards you, then this excessive and obsessive behaviour provides a useful context to explain the reason for your behaviour.

But you would still need to have demonstrated that, despite his behaviour, you made reasonable steps to make arrangements for him to have contact with your child, and that he failed to have contact on the dates and occasions you mention.

Essentially, you need to show that you have thought about your child's needs to have contact with him and acted consistent with those needs, by offering him dates for contact.

Always think about your child's needs and put them first. It does not matter whether you think the other parent is useless, or a poor role model, you are not your child.

As I hope is now very clear to you, there is a lot of work, planning and preparation involved when giving evidence at court.

It is thus a huge mistake for you to attend court and go in to the witness box, without having taken the time to thoroughly read all the information before the court and, after digesting all the information, diligently prepare to give evidence.

Let us suppose you are attending court because you have separated from the mother or father of your child, and are unable to agree decisions such as who your child lives with, or details in connection with how much time your child spends with you and the other parent.

It is not sufficient just to read and familiarise yourself with the detail of your case. You also need to know in detail, the contents of your ex-partner's court statements, claims and arguments, and in the light of their case, to decide on how you will answer questions that are likely to be addressed to you.

If you do not know the detail of your ex-partner's case, how can you hope to answer any questions appropriately when fired at you in the witness box? **You must plan and prepare diligently before attending court.**

Something you must continue to bear in mind, is that your decisions, behaviour, attitude, written and verbal responses, are all under the spotlight of scrutiny, once the court becomes involved with the life of your family. So if you neglect to address your mind to pertinent information in your ex- partner's evidence, then it really presents the court with the impression that you are not sufficiently interested in your court case and the outcome regarding your child.

The judge, your opposing barrister, or lawyer and any other professional, such as the court appointed Children's Guardian (from CAFCASS) are not just vigilant concerning what you omit to do. They are equally observant in connection, with the actions you choose to take. **So, choose to have a good attitude.**

Invariably in cases where one, or both parents have found it necessary to involve the courts in their private law dispute, one or both of the parents are angry, or antagonistic towards the other.

This is not a behaviour you can afford to commit, or in the case of your ex behaving with hostility towards you, it is not in your interests, or your child's interests, to be seen to retaliate, or rise to provocation directed towards you.

Now, I know that in the real world you might choose to respond by fighting fire with fire, but there are at least two reasons why this would not be in your best interests. Firstly, and most importantly, if you behave in this way, your child is likely to be harmed in some way, as children do not like to see or hear their parents arguing or fighting, and there is much evidence that this causes children harm.

Secondly, and related to the first point, if you do not show the necessary self-control, it will be noted, and this will not work in your favour during the court process.

You may now be thinking to yourself, that it was your ex-partner who began behaving antagonistically towards you, so why is it okay for them to behave in that way towards you, don't the same rules apply to them?

The answer to that question is yes they do, but that is not, and should not be your first concern. Your first concern should be to demonstrate, that your overriding responsibility is to act consistently with whatever is in the best interests of your child.

You cannot demonstrate that you are acting in your child's best interests, by showing your anger and hostility to your ex-partner or anyone else at court. **So, do not show anger, do not swear, instead practise calmness and cooperation.**

The manner in which your ex-partner behaves, is his or her choice, they may not realise that their hostile and inappropriate behaviour is harming their child and their case. Or they may simply not be able to manage or regulate their emotions in such a way as to demonstrate their ability to remain focused on your child's wellbeing.

Whatever the reason, your ex-partner chooses to behave abusively, is a matter for them to deal with or consider. Your role, during the entire court proceedings (not just whilst in the witness box) is to do this: **demonstrate your ability to be a good parent, and act throughout in accordance with your child's best interests.**

What you should seek to avoid at all costs is **getting into 'tit for tat' or competitive behaviour with your former partner.** This type of behaviour is never helpful to any parent because it puts you in a very negative light.

Remember to keep this following statement, stapled uppermost in your consciousness: "The judge does not know you at all. The only knowledge they have of you, is what is documented in the court bundle and the way you behave in his or her presence."

Bear in mind also, that judges are used to seeing parents in private law family cases being vituperative and hostile to one another, and as they repeatedly view this, it is easy to lump both parents together, and see them as equally as bad as one another.

This is not the impression you, want to leave with the Judge, or the appointed CAFCASS officer.

I also wish to be careful here not to give you, what I consider to be an incorrect impression. The Judge sees cases such as yours, before him or her several times a day, on a daily basis. Thus, there are so many cases, that the courts are inundated and, in my view, what this means is that they do not have the time to allocate to your case, or any other private law family case, the amount of time I believe they really deserve.

Given this reality, I would argue it is in your best interests, to try to **stand out** from the crowd, or at the very least, do whatever is required to avoid being lumped together with parents who fail to show that they have the ability to consistently put their child's needs first.

At this point, a few questions may be surfacing in your mind, that may require clarification, and please forgive me if some of what I document here is common knowledge to you, or seems to be (since readers of this book will be at differing stages of knowledge or understanding).

I mentioned earlier in this chapter, how imperative it was to have fully read, and digested, not just the information in your statement/s, but also the information provided by your ex-partner, as well as any reports from CAFCASS, or other professionals.

The reason I have stressed this, is because I believe you need to begin to see things, not just from your perspective. If you are to give yourself the optimum chance of giving great evidence at court (and giving yourself the best chance of attaining a favourable outcome) **you have to begin to develop the ability to have what I would refer to as a 'macro-view,'** as opposed to a 'micro-view' of your family law matter.

Developing this ability to see your case on a macro level, is akin to viewing the matter more objectively, like a judge might view it, viewing your case more objectively, from a higher vantage point.

I have probably bored you to death, talking about the importance of being able to see things from your child's viewpoint, and I make no apology for doing so, because if you're going to be seen as able to place your child's needs before your own, it is imperative that you can do this.

Whilst giving evidence you need to show or demonstrate empathy. Show the court by what you say and the way you behave, that you have the insight to understand how your child feels and that you can, and will act in accordance with what's best for them, having taken their wishes and feelings into account.

You need to show that your child is at the forefront of your mind and thoughts, not just once in a while, but consistently.

So when you answer questions, when you make decisions, your actions and behaviour should demonstrate that you **prioritise your child's wishes and feelings**.

Now this does not mean that you always do everything your child wants. Not at all. It means having taken the time to know what is in your child's best interests, and what is not in their best interests, that you **show balance, flexibility, sensitivity, discipline, responsibility and guidance** in the way you answer questions related to the care you offer your child.

In order to be able to do this, you have to have a fairly clear understanding of the types of situations that cause harm to your child and are thus not in your child's best interests, as opposed to the sorts of things that positively result in your child thriving, and developing appropriately in all areas.

Although this is not a book specialising on parenting, if you are to present well in your statements, and combine that with presenting congruently whilst giving evidence, you have to have at least a reasonable understanding about what constitutes good parenting.

Your ideas about what is good parenting, from what is not will differ, dependent upon your own experiences of being parented, and this is very largely, the yardstick by which you gauge parenting.

The judge and the courts however, are guided for the most part by professionals, such as psychiatrists, psychologists and social workers in determining what is seen to be harmful, as opposed to what is believed to constitute good practice in terms of parenting.

It is now well known, for example, that children are harmed by being exposed to conflict, domestic violence or abuse, between parents or caregivers. When children are first exposed to fights, or domestic abuse, they are petrified by it, but if it occurs on a regular basis, after continual exposure, they become used to it, and eventually begin to see it as normal behaviour.

If your child is frequently exposed to arguments and domestic violence, apart from the risk of him being physically hurt during the altercation, there are a number of ways in which their emotional development will be negatively impacted, which if not corrected will have a 'knock on effect' during his childhood and throughout his adult life.

Now, that may sound obvious to you, but if you have been raised by a parent, or parents who have regularly engaged, throughout your childhood in abusing each other, you may have become de-sensitised to this type of behaviour. It may have become 'normal' to you, and you will then be less likely to demonstrate the level of empathy your child might need.

If you have been brought up by a parent, or parents who have had alcohol, or drug addictions, unless you have gone out of your way to address the effect of such influences on you, the chances are, that you may likely have a 'blind spot' in this area, and so may have difficulty acknowledging the risk you may unwittingly expose your child to.

The same would be true, in the event that you grew up, with parents or carers who kept you off, or away from school frequently, or who had no issue with you being allowed to stay up, into the early hours of the morning, watching adult movies, whilst you were clearly under age and required a full night's sleep, in order to be ready for school the next morning.

If this was your experience, it might mean that you are not too concerned when your child misses the odd day of school here and there, tends to arrive at school late, or behaves inappropriately at school, having watched programmes with adult content.

It could be that you were raised by parents who, for whatever reason, had no issue with you being cared for by multiple carers, or living in an environment which was unclean, messy or barely habitable.

In the event that these were the circumstances in which you were raised, there is a likelihood that you may not recognise if your child is living in an inappropriate or neglectful home environment. It has nothing to do with not caring for or loving your child, instead it is a reflection of the parental influences you were continually exposed to as a child.

I am hoping that you are beginning to grasp the reality, that there is no such thing as 'perfect parenting.' I have, above, just picked out a handful of ways in which your child could be being cared for in a harmful way, but there are many other ways which could be identified.

So you are probably wondering now, what the relevance of these discussions about parenting have to do with you giving evidence well at court. The point is simply this, if there are aspects to your ability to parent, which are either incongruent with your written or verbal evidence, then that represents a large chink in your armour, which your ex-partner's lawyer will happily expose, and capitalise on when you are giving evidence.

I am mentioning this to you, because you need to think through everything you have stated, and everything in your ex-partner's statement (including any other reports from professionals) that highlights or suggests any deficiency or shortcoming, on your part, with regard to the way you parent.

In my view, this may be difficult for you to do, for two main reasons, one of which I have already alluded to:

It will be difficult for you, if you have been brought up in a certain way, it will not be easy for you to see, or understand why certain parenting decisions may not be in your child's best interests. Again, this is not because you do not love your child. Loving your child however, does not preclude you, or anyone else, from unconsciously behaving in ways that can result in your child being harmed.

Secondly, every parent, and that includes me as well as you, would want to believe that we are good parents. The reality is that if you tried, you would search long and hard, to find parents who willingly put their hands up, and admit that they are 'bad parents.'

What this means is, you will need to be open or far more open, than perhaps you have been up until now. Just to be clear with you, I am not trying to make a judgement about your character or personality.

That would be foolish, as I do not know you, but what I do know, and understand very well, is that how you have been parented over the years, represents a constant, repetitive pattern of care, that is so much a part of who you are by the time you are an adult, that it is what you now see as very normal parental behaviour.

Even if, as an adult you recognise, from your knowledge of how other people have been cared for that some aspect of your parenting was faulty in some way, it will be very difficult without consistent help and support for you to fully appreciate any shortcoming you may have in this area.

The important thing is to **be open in connection with parenting** and just as advised, when discussing the necessity of developing a good or positive attitude, it may prove helpful to use the assistance of friends in raising your awareness in this area.

Don't ask, or talk to people who you know will tell you what you may want to hear. Talk to people who have successfully brought up their children, and ask them, not just about the things that worked for them as parents, but also the things that didn't work. Ask them about the ways in which they failed spectacularly and their regrets.

You can learn as much, perhaps more from people's experiences of failing at parenting, as you can from people's successes; but both are important.

I have added this discussion about parenting in this chapter, because it is so important, in terms of how you present throughout the evidence you give prior to attending and during your attendance at court.

So this brief discussion on your insight concerning parenting, is obviously something you will need to do, long before you arrive at court to give evidence, but I have repeated the necessity of you doing so, due to its significance, in connection with how you present at court.

When giving evidence, one final thing to be aware of, is that if you have to stop giving evidence for a while, due to the court breaking for lunch, **do not talk to anyone during that lunch hour.** Isolate yourself from others, so as to preclude any accusation that you discussed the case or evidence with anyone during that time. The judge will warn you about this, in any event. If you break for lunch or the court day ends, before you complete giving your evidence, the same rule applies. You are not allowed to talk to anyone, about the case until you finish giving your evidence.

Key Learning Points

- Turn your mobile phone off before you go into the court.
- If the question asked of you is beyond your knowledge or expertise, say so. Do not try to

answer it. If you were not there at the time, or if you are asked a question suitable for a psychologist and you are a social worker, it is only wise, not to attempt to answer it.

- Do not ask the lawyer questions, that is not your role.
- Be prepared to be led by the judge at all times
- When answering questions, give your attention to the judge.
- Ask the judge if you can use your notes to refresh your memory. The judge may allow this if, they were notes made contemporaneously.
- Do not be overawed by the judge. Remain able to put over your views and responses, and if you make a mistake, say so as soon as it occurs to you.
- Be assertive when required, but not aggressive.
- Do not react or retaliate, practise calmness and cooperation.
- Do not compete, instead stand out from the crowd, be a 'breath of fresh air,' by exemplifying a great state of mind, focused only on your child.

- If you have to stop giving evidence for lunch break, or at the end of the day. You are not allowed to talk to any of the people involved in the case, until you conclude giving your evidence.

Conclusion

Giving evidence at court as a parent, is probably one of the most pressurised and stressful experiences you are likely to ever face. It involves you mastering your emotions, accepting responsibility for your current circumstances, and developing and maintaining a positive attitude throughout.

It will undoubtedly take up much of your time, learning new information, planning, preparing and mentally rehearsing new, essential habits.

But if you follow the principles or guidance I have outlined above, particularly in the preceding chapter, and practise doing so repeatedly, you will optimise your chances of being perceived as a credible witness and of attaining the outcome you require.

I am fully aware that many of the ways, and attitudes of mind I have strongly urged you to adopt, are likely alien and uncomfortable to you, currently.

However, I would ask you to consider the following points:

Firstly, there is a reason you are at this point of needing to go to the family court and that reason is because something has gone wrong in your life, and is impacting or has the potential to impact, on the wellbeing of your children.

Secondly, if you take the time to analyse, whatever has gone wrong in your family life, and are honest with yourself (as opposed to blaming another or others) you will accept that the principles, or guidance I am recommending to you, are sound.

You will appreciate that behaving courteously, putting yourself in others shoes, accepting your share of responsibility, praising others instead of criticising or blaming them, and admitting when, and where you were in the wrong, for instance; are principles that if adopted, would likely have circumvented the current circumstances.

Of course, I realise a relationship involves at least two people and it would be nice if others adopted, these same principles towards you too. But you can only take responsibility for your, own attitudes and behaviour.

If you did not know better before, you do now!

Thirdly, the adoption of these principles, are not just vital for court and giving evidence, they are vital for you throughout your life to help you achieve happiness, harmony and success, within all of your relationships, including of course, those with your children.

So, it really is in your best interests, to try them out and utilise them in your life, from now on. Let your court case be a great motivating influence, to form new habits that work in your interest, as opposed to against them.

Whether you are a parent, attending court due to involvement in a private law case or a parent involved in public law care proceedings, one would have to be devoid of feeling, to be unable to recognise that your experience is inevitably one steeped in emotion, distress, hurt and frustration.

These emotions are invariably intensified, by the adversarial nature of court, and its process, which very probably results in parents who are already vulnerable, feeling isolated, unsupported, criticised, abused and uncared for.

Whilst you may not always recognise my attitude to you or your particular circumstances, as sensitive or sympathetic, I hope that you are nevertheless, able to understand and value the information gathered in this book and put it to good use in your court case.

What you and I have to be aware of, especially when in the heights of distress, is that sometimes what we hear as criticism or as unsympathetic, is helpful support, that we have yet to recognise in that light.

At the beginning of the book I explained, I was a social worker, and that being the case, I remain highly conscious of the negative views that parents and society hold concerning them.

However, you may not realise it, but when social workers in public law cases bring a case to court, their knowledge, behaviour, attitudes, reputation and practice are also exposed, and on the line.

Of course the stakes for you, as a parent are much higher, considering matters such as the placement of your child is at risk. But nevertheless, the stakes for social workers are high, since you could lose your livelihood and reputation, if deemed to perform unsuitably or to demonstrate what is considered to be very poor practice.

This reality sets up circumstances, in which people act to do their job, to protect children to the best of their ability, but that also includes protecting themselves, as best they can. By the time your case is in court, the lines of demarcation are drawn, and you as a parent, are on one side and your children's social worker is on the other side.

It then becomes a very difficult exercise to navigate a path, in giving evidence that is required of you, in what you consider is in the best interests of the child, whilst being at the same time, supportive and empathic to parents.

I have mentioned the above, in the hope that it helps you, to recognise that for social workers, the popular belief held by some parents that they enjoy taking people's children away, is for the vast majority of social workers, simply unreal.

The reason it is highly unlikely to be the case is because, not only do social workers have to go through the rigours of giving evidence, but they have in addition, a mountain of paper work to complete, whenever a case is taken to court, and social workers are definitely not short of work.

My reason in sharing this information with you, is to hopefully raise your awareness of these realities and perhaps play a part in making you more receptive to the concerns related to your parenting.

If you are a social worker, I hope this book provides you, with extra knowledge, skills and tips to assist you in giving your evidence in the family court. It is a shame that social workers generally receive little or insufficient training, on how to give evidence, and cope adequately with cross-examination.

As I stated at the beginning of this book, lawyers receive training on cross-examination. I think it is unwise and unfair, that social workers are not equally well prepared to cope with what is expected of them at the family court.

The lack of support social workers receive in this respect is, I consider, a further reflection of the way social workers are perceived and valued.

Your role is complex and onerous enough, without being subjected to giving evidence in the absence of adequate training and support in this key area.

As social workers and managers of social workers, there has to be an appreciation and acknowledgement, that giving evidence is not only stressful, but traumatising, particularly when you are inexperienced.

Even when you are an experienced practitioner, you can and are likely to encounter complex, demanding cases, which evoke all kinds of emotions, and reactions within you. Giving evidence in cases such as these, always has the potential to give rise to long lasting distress.

I have written this book to help both parents and social workers gain the knowledge, skills and tips to adequately defend themselves at court.

I hope this book goes a long way in arming you with the advice and information you need. It cannot meet every need, but I hope it is, for you, a great start.

Michael D. Watson.

Essential Giving Evidence Checklist

As a thank you for purchasing a copy of my book, you have also gained free access to my Essential Giving Evidence Checklist.

This essential checklist is designed to help you:

1. Prepare more thoroughly

2. Present more competently and more confidently.

3. Give more focused answers

4. To recognise it is imperative to master your emotions

You can download this vital checklist today at the following link: www.familycourttips.co.uk

Profile

Michael is a professionally qualified social worker with over 3 decades of experience working with children and families within the family court. He has 30 years firsthand experience of giving evidence in the family court. He has also supported and prepared parents for court hearings.

This is his second book, the first one is titled 'How To Represent Yourself In Family Court.'

After years of seeing families and colleagues endure the ordeal of giving evidence with little or preparation or support, Michael felt empowered to utilise his extensive knowledge and experience in the industry, to write this book to help those going through this harrowing process, to improve their understanding regarding giving evidence and greatly increase their opportunity of obtaining a satisfactory outcome at court.

Printed in Great Britain
by Amazon

80410482R00190